CRYSTALLIZING

PUBLIC OPINION

CRYSTALLIZING
PUBLIC OPINION

EDWARD L. BERNAYS

NEW YORK, NY

Printed in the United States of America
10 9 8 7 6 5

Ig Publishing
Box 2547
New York, NY 10163
www.igpub.com

Library of Congress Cataloging-in-Publication Data

Bernays, Edward L., 1891-1995.
 Crystallizing public opinion / Edward L. Bernays.
    p. cm.
 Reprint. Originally published by Boni and Liveright in 1923.
 Includes bibliographical references.
 ISBN 978-1-935439-26-4
 1. Public opinion. 2. Social psychology. 3. Publicity. I.
Title.
 HM1236.B47 2011
 303.3'8--dc23
                                        2011025346

To My Wife

CONTENTS

PART III—TECHNIQUE AND METHOD

PART IV—ETHICAL RELATIONS

INTRODUCTION

I first learned of Edward Bernays in the late 1960s, while I was a graduate student in history beginning to investigate the social roots of American consumer culture. As I read through his writings, I started to grasp his largely unknown influence on the contours of contemporary life. While his life story stood, for the most part, in the shadows of American history, this was "the invisible wire puller" who had devised many of the powerful ways that the tools of mass persuasion would shape the terrain of American society from the early twentieth century onward.[1]

Beginning his career in the early 1900s, Bernays would soon become one of the most influential pioneers of American public relations, a person whose worldly activities, though not widely known, left a deep mark on the configuration of our world.

Today all of this has changed. Due to a growing interest in the historical relationship between media, culture and society in the modern age, the name of Edward Bernays has become more and more familiar. Since the 1970s, an increasing number of books and films have appeared, and this once covert PR operative has been transformed into an his-torical figure of controversy and renown.[2]

Born in Vienna in 1891, Bernays was the double nephew of Sigmund Freud. His mother was Freud's elder sister, Anna;

his father Ely was Freud's wife's (Martha Bernays Freud) brother. His family background impressed him with the enormous power of intellectual life and accustomed him to the privileges and creature comforts of bourgeois existence.

Bernays was also a farsighted architect of modern propaganda techniques who, dramatically, from the early 1920s—when *Crystallizing Public Opinion* first appeared—helped to consolidate a fateful marriage between theories of mass and individual psychology and the designs of corporate and political persuasion.

During the First World War, Bernays served as a foot soldier for the U.S. Committee on Public Information (CPI)—the vast American propaganda machine mobilized in 1917 to package, advertise and sell the war as one that would "Make the World Safe for Democracy." The CPI would become the source from which marketing strategies for subsequent wars—including the spurious and deadly adventure in Iraq—would flow.

In the twenties, Bernays fathered the link between corporate sales campaigns and popular social causes, when—while working for the American Tobacco Company—he persuaded women's rights marchers in New York City to hold up Lucky Strike cigarettes as symbolic "Torches of Freedom." In October of 1929, Bernays also originated the now familiar "global media event," when he dreamed up "Light's Golden Jubilee," a world-wide celebratory spectacle honoring the fiftieth anniversary of the electric light bulb, sponsored—behind the scenes—by the General Electric Corporation.

Bernays's influence would continue to hold sway well into the post-World War II era. To put it simply, Bernays's career—more than that of any other individual—roughed out what have become the strategies and practices of public relations in the United States and, increasingly, on a global scale.

Alongside the numerous, well-documented campaigns he directed—including one for the United Fruit Company which led to the 1954 CIA-engineered coup that overthrew the democratically elected president of Guatemala—Bernays wrote prolifically.[3] His books, *Crystallizing Public Opinion* (1923), *Propaganda* (1928), and his seminal 1947 article, "The Engineering of Consent," are among the most significant documents in the history of what one scholar has termed, "the compliance professions," those groups and often clandestine organizations that exist to manufacture public thought, opinion and be-havior on behalf of political and corporate clients.[4]

Propaganda, and "The Engineering of Consent," were the self-confident and unabashed writings of a man who was already established as the foremost figure in the public relations fraternity. Both are filled with bold and hyperbolic proclamations, exemplified by the opening paragraph in *Propaganda*.

> The conscious and intelligent manipulation of the organized habits and opinions of the masses is an important element in democratic society. Those who manipulate this unseen mechanism of society constitute an invisible govern-ment which is the true ruling power of our country.[5]

In 1923, however, Bernays urgently believed that a case for the practices of public relations in a democratic society still needed to be made. *Crystallizing Public Opinion* was his presentation of this case, a straightforward manifesto providing a measured and studious argument for the importance of a new profession, which he dubbed "the public relations counsel." Much as legal counsels advise and defend clients in the realm of law—the public relations counsel, as Bernays described him—it was always a he—provided expertise to clients on ways to effectively mold public opinion on behalf of their interests. The rise of this new profession, he contended, had already begun to alter the social landscape.

> No single profession…within the last ten years has extended its field of usefulness more remarkably and touched upon intimate and important aspects of the everyday life of the world more significantly than the profession of public relations counsel.

Bernays's insistence on the importance of defining public relations as a respectable profession was founded on his belief that many people looked upon the practices of publicity with disdain. In this book, Bernays sought to redeem the reputation of public relations and situate it as the intrinsic outcome of a serious intellectual tradition. In naming the book, he drew upon the language of science. "Crystallization," in the field of physical chemistry, describes the process by which an amorphous entity—a gas or suspension in fluid form—is transformed into a solid coherent mass. For Bernays, "crystallizing public opinion" was about taking an "ill-defined, mercurial and changeable group of individual judgments" and transforming them into a cohesive and manageable form.

In the book, Bernays portrayed the public relations practitioner as an instrumental social scientist, a resolute student of human motivation. "His text books for this study are the facts of life," he claimed, the "mental equipment of the average individual."

The public relations counsel, he argued, specialized in understanding the public mind and knowing how to create those circumstances that would gain public attention to consolidate public opinion. A pivotal aspect of the PR counsel's "wide range of instruments and techniques," as Bernays described them, was an intimate knowledge of those "mediums… through which public attention is reached and influenced. … the channels of thought and communication." In addition to his discussions of newspapers, magazines and the recent development of broadcast radio, Bernays's description of those "channels of thought and communication" included word-of-mouth networks and the role played by individuals whose opinions influence the outlooks of others—teachers, business leaders, the clergy, etc.

If understanding the dynamics of public opinion was one of his specialties, so too was a comprehension of the railroad tracks along which ideas and opinions travel. An early look at his flair for unseen engineering is found in the work he did in 1913 to foster the success of a controversial play, entitled "Damaged Goods," which dealt with the controversial topic of syphilis. This was a time, Bernays wrote in the book that follows, when sexual matters of any kind were not considered appropriate for public discussion. As Bernays noted, "Anthony Comstock, who headed the New York Society for the Suppression of Vice, had already closed other shows that he thought too daring."

In order to bypass such Victorian prudery, Bernays created a new organization and enlisted the public support of "men and women whose good faith was beyond question and would be responsive to our cause." Turning "Damaged Goods" into a dramatic brief on behalf of public health these men and women—who included John D. Rockefeller, Jr.; Simon Flexner, the head of the Rockefeller Institute for Medical Research; Rose Pastor Stokes, an eminent social worker, and Mrs. William

K. Vanderbilt, among others—transformed a potential failure into a major success that eventually gained national press when performed at the White House for President Woodrow Wilson and his high profile guests. In handling publicity for the play, Bernays displayed an uncommon genius social engineering that would define his career and would sharpen the focus of public relations thinking from then on.

Beyond his discussion of the "Damaged Goods" campaign, and other vivid case studies, *Crystallizing Public Opinion* was Bernays's response to changes that had taken place in American society in the decades preceding its publication. Bernays wrote of the extent to which upper class Americans who had formerly "stood aloof from the general public and were able to say 'The public be damned,'" had come to recognize that such open contempt wasn't playing well in Peoria, or anywhere else. Social unrest, and widespread anti-business activism were its most visible consequences. "The willingness to spend thousands of dollars in obtaining professional advice on how best to present one's views or products to a public is based on this fact."

• • •

As this book clearly reveals, Bernays was building on ideas that had been percolating in Europe and the United States for several decades. Unlike his later writings, which paid lip service to his intellectual forebears, in *Crystallizing Public Opinion*, Bernays built his arguments on a foundation of ideas culled from a variety of prominent commentators on politics, society and the dynamics of psychic life. Their presence is manifest throughout the book.

Of course there was his uncle, Sigmund Freud, whose theories regarding the unconscious, the power of symbols, and the subterranean meaning of dreams had gained currency in the United States by the 1920s. But in reading Bernays's book, it is evident that other thinkers were also extremely important to his worldview.

Though his name does not appear in *Crystallizing Public Opinion*, perhaps the most influential precursor to Bernays's writings and approach—whom he named in later writings—was the French sociologist, Gustave Le Bon, who in 1895 published *The Crowd: A Study of the Popular Mind*.

Le Bon's book was translated into nineteen languages within a year, and soon gained a wide readership among Western elites. It inspired the creation of what would become the rapidly growing field of Social Psychology, a field that continues to prosper. Le Bon was less concerned with public opinion than he was with the rapid growth of democratic movements, and the threat they posed to the established hierarchies of power. In his book, he proposed to offer a diagnostic anatomy of the mind of the masses, believing that a "knowledge of the psychology of crowds is today the last resource of the statesman...."

In *The Crowd* Le Bon provided a preliminary handbook for people interested in "managing the human climate," offering advice on the usefulness of images and theatrics as tools of persuasion, and making continual reference to the unconscious powers of suggestion. While Le Bon's book offered little in the way of practical advice, his general estimation of the popular mind—that it was driven not by reason, but by illogical and primitive instinctive forces— would profoundly influence subsequent engineers of consent for decades to come. "Crowds have always undergone the influence of illusions," he wrote, "Whoever can supply them with illusions is easily their master. Whoever attempts to destroy their illusions is always their victim." For Le Bon, to exert control over the social order in a democratic age a "small intellectual aristocracy," adept in the application of mass psychology, was essential.

Following Le Bon, a growing number of Western thinkers began to wrestle with the mechanisms that generated mass perception. Le Bon's close friend, Gabriel Tarde, wrote of the extent to which newspapers, and other early mass media, contributed to a kind of groupthink. Tarde suggested in 1898 that "the public" was the "social group of the future," and that its private thoughts and discussions were but a product of the public power of the press, and international news services, which were providing an increasingly homogenized picture of reality.

> The press unifies and invigorates conversations… every morning the papers give their public the conversations of the day…This increasing similarity of simultaneous conversations in an ever more vast geographic domain is one of the most important characteristics of our time.

Evoking a metaphor inspired by the recent invention of the phonograph, Tarde argued, "the conversations of individuals… are forced to follow the groove of their borrowed thoughts. One pen suffices to set off a million tongues." This perspective, as you will find in *Crystallizing Public Opinion*, infused Bernays's understanding of how the public relations counsel does his work, particularly in his analysis of the social and personal channels of communication.

Others whose work influenced Bernays included the British political scientist, Graham Wallas, whose 1908 book, *Human Nature in Politics*, maintained that "the empirical art of politics " was not based on fact-based appeals to reason. Instead, he asserted, it "consists largely in the creation of opinion, by the deliberate exploitation of subconscious, non-rational inference."

In *Crystallizing Public Opinion*, Bernays repeatedly cites a 1916 book, *The Instincts of the Herd in Peace and War*. Written by the British surgeon and social psychologist Wilfred Trotter (whom Bernays erroneously refers to as William Trotter), who maintained:

> No understanding of the causes of stability and instability in human society is possible until the undiminished vigour of instincts in man is fully recognized.

Of particular interest to Trotter, and to Bernays, was the "herd instinct," the unceasing need to gain the approval and camaraderie of the social group. The individual Trotter wrote, is "more sensitive to the voice of the herd than to any other influence. It can inhibit or stimulate his thought and conduct.

> It is the source of his moral codes, of the sanctions of his ethics and philosophy. It can endow him with energy, courage, and endurance, and can as easily take these away.

For Edward Bernays, these early writings, and others cited in this book, provided a psychic architecture that a public relations practitioner needed to understand in great depth. Without a thorough comprehension of the unconscious and instinctual triggers that stimulate human behavior, he would argue throughout his long career, the work of the "public relations counsel" would be impossible.

In many ways, the experience of the First World War challenged many mainstream intellectuals' faith in the possibility of direct democracy. The propaganda efforts of the CPI reinforced a growing belief that ordinary men and women were incapable of rational thought. For democracy to work effectively, public opinion needed to be guided by what historian Robert Westbrook has characterized as "enlightened and responsible elites."

More than any other individual, the prominent and powerful journalist, writer, and confidant of Presidents—Walter Lippmann—propagated this idea. A former socialist, Lippmann had moved, even before the war, to the conviction that popular sovereignty was impossible in the "Great Society," his catchphrase for the modern world. As the United States entered "The Great War" in 1917, Lippmann played a pivotal role in convincing President Woodrow Wilson to deploy a vast propaganda bureau designed to deflect widespread skepticism and bring public opinion on board.

After the war, Lippmann held fast to the idea that the American people were incapable of self-rule. For democracy to work, the machinery of the public mind needed to be understood and managed by an educated elite. This idea was central to Lippmann's pivotal book, *Public Opinion*, whose influence is evident in the title, and throughout the pages, of Bernays's *Crystallizing Public Opinion*, which appeared the following year.

Lippmann's *Public Opinion* remains one of the most important books of the twentieth century. Its diagnosis of "the public mind," along with its ideas about how leaders can manage it, remains the most articulate statement regarding the exercise of power in the United States on to the present, and underlined the critical importance of what Lippmann termed "the manufacture of consent."

Two of Lippmann's ideas were particularly significant as Bernays crafted the job of the "public relations counsel." The first of these was Lippmann's argument that people's view of reality was guided by the "pictures in their heads." Living within the cocoons of their personal lives, and with minimal direct access to the outer world, most people's sense of reality was shaped by what he termed "pseudo-environments." While this meant that ordinary citizens were not able to intelligently comprehend the real issues of their world, their reliance on pseudo-environments provided educated elites with a powerful tool for effective leadership.

"The new psychology...the study of dreams, fantasies and rationalizations, has thrown light on how the pseudo-environment is put together," he wrote. If patterns of perception could be unearthed, if scientists could uncover the "habits" of people's eyes, they might also learn to engineer "pseudo-environments" which could persuade people to see their "larger political environment...more successfully." Perception management, he contended, would defend democracy from the prospect of capricious authoritarianism.

> Though it is itself an irrational force, the power of
> public opinion might be placed at the disposal of those
> who stood for workable law as against brute assertion.

A second idea that stands conspicuously within Bernays' thinking, was Lippmann's introduction of the modern usage of the word stereotype. Prior to the twenties, stereotype was a term relating to the printing trades, but Lippmann redefined it, describing stereotypes as a "repertory of fixed impressions" that "we carry around in our heads," rigid mental templates that frame individual experience in an increasingly anonymous world.

For Lippmann, stereotypes did not emanate from the individual, but were an inexorable by-product of their surrounding culture, a perceptual reflex that imposed itself between people's eyes and the world they believed they were seeing.

> For the most part we do not first see, and then define, we define first and then see. In the great blooming, buzzing confusion of the outer world we pick out what our culture has already defined for us, and we tend to perceive that which we have picked out in the form stereotyped for us by our culture.

Ensemble, Lippmann argued, stereotypes constituted a coherent—if inaccurate—worldview. Unconsciously, but aggressively, people relied on them for a sense of where they belong in the world.

> These preconceptions, unless education has made us acutely aware, governs deeply the whole process of perception. They mark out certain objects as familiar or strange, emphasizing the difference, so that slightly familiar is seen as very familiar, and the somewhat strange is sharply alien.

As central components of people's mental equipment, Lippmann described stereotypes as the "foundations" of their "universe."

> They are an ordered, more or less consistent picture of the world...They may not be a complete picture...but they are a picture of a possible world to which we are adapted. In that world people and things have their

well-known places, and do certain expected things. We feel at home there. We fit in. We are members. We know the way around. There we find the charm of the familiar, the normal, the dependable; its grooves and shapes are where we are accustomed to find them… It fits as snugly as an old shoe.

Given the comfort that this "repertory of stereotypes" affords us, he concluded,

…[A]ny disturbance of the stereotypes seems like an attack on the founda-tions of the universe. It is an attack on the foundations of our universe, and, where big things are at stake, we do not readily admit that there is any difference between our universe and the universe.

As Bernays was writing *Crystallizing Public Opinion*, the logic of Lippmann's book infused his mind and his argument. "The public relations counsel creates new stereotypes," he wrote, building these stereotypes out of a keen understanding of the "fundamental instincts in the people he is trying to reach."

The public relations specialist's goal was to create "a compact, vivid simplification of complicated issues." This idea drew upon Lippmann's theories about the anatomy of public opinion, along with the conclusions of a battery of social psychologists that preceded him.

Describing the peculiar aptitude of the public relations counsel, Bernays maintained "it is his capacity for crystallizing the obscure tendencies of the public mind before they have reached definite expression, which makes him so valuable."

His ability to create those symbols to which the public is ready to respond; his ability to know and to analyze those reactions which the public is ready to give; his ability to find those stereotypes, individual and community, which will bring favorable responses; his ability to speak the language of his audience and to receive from it a favorable reception are his contributions. The appeal to the instincts and the universal desires is the basic method through which he produces his results.

In light of this kind of professionalized necromancy, Bernays was careful to insert the notion that the "public relations counsel" must closely adhere to ethical standards. Manipulating mass perception is always a dodgy exercise, but without a backbone of ethics, even Bernays was aware that it could be used towards dangerous ends.

There is one danger in the use of stereotypes by the public relations counsel. That... demagogues in every field of social relationship can take advantage of the public.

At the end of the day, the counsel's intellectual arsenal had one primary purpose: the manufacture of news. "The public relations counsel must not only supply news—he must create news."

This didn't happen by dropping off press releases at newspaper or other media offices. It came instead from an educated ability to understand "what news actually is"—what it looks and tastes like—and the capacity to orchestrate occurrences that will attract news coverage and be viewed by the public as current events.

> The public relations counsel must lift startling facts
> from his whole subject and present them as news. He
> must isolate ideas and develop them into events so
> that they can be more readily understood and so they
> can claim attention as news.

Throughout *Crystallizing*, Bernays cited numerous examples drawn from his own practice, to exemplify this process in vivid. This is key to the durable relevance of this book: its effective, if somewhat disturbing, amalgamation of contemporary theory with what have become standard practices.

In recent times, the persistent belief that President Barack Obama was not born in the United States, and therefore was ineligible to become President, offers a prime example of the extent to which the assertion of "startling facts" can become and remain news for years—even when empirical evidence demonstrates that these facts are wholly fictitious. As Lippmann wrote, people will vehemently cling to the stereotypes that comprise the foundation of their universe, even when they are patently erroneous.

• • •

In writing the introduction to Edward Bernays's *Crystallizing Public Opinion*, I would be remiss not to mention my lengthy personal encounter with Bernays, twenty years after I had first encountered his writings. It was remarkable.

In two of my earliest books, *Captains of Consciousness* (1976) and *All Consuming Images* (1988) Bernays had appeared as a central character, an eloquent and influential ideologue of American consumer culture, and a founding father in the field of public relations.

Both times my encounters with Bernays were like those that usually take place between historians and the "historical figures" that they write about. They were exchanges between old documents and the inquiring mind of a reader and interpreter.

When, in 1990, as I commenced work on *PR! A Social History of Spin* (1996), I assumed, reasonably, that Bernays was long gone. The picturesque record that he had left behind was as close as I was likely to get to him. Soon, however, I stumbled onto the fact that my reasonable assumption was incorrect. In a conversation with a neighbor of mine named Richard Weiner—who was himself a prominent member of the public relations fraternity, and remains a prolific author on communications issues—I learned that Bernays was, in fact, still alive approaching his hundredth birthday. In fact he resided in Cambridge, Massachusetts, only a short walk from the Widener Library at Harvard where I had first discovered some of his writings more than twenty years earlier.

When he heard about the book I was working on, Weiner instructed me: "If you are going to do this book, you've got to talk to Eddie Bernays." I was astonished and delighted to hear Bernays referred to in the present tense; I was also amused to hear him referred to as "Eddie." Behind the aura of an historical figure, stood a guy called Eddie. I obtained Bernays' telephone number and set out to arrange an interview.

An exploratory call to Bernays reached an answering machine. A woman's voice, official in tone, informed me that I had reached the offices of "Dr. Edward L. Bernays," and that "Dr. Bernays" was currently unavailable. I was instructed to leave a message. For a man of almost 100, Bernays was still communicating an air of business-as-usual. I told the machine:

My name is Stuart Ewen. I am an historian, a writer. I'm

currently working on a book on the social history of public relations. I would very much like to come to Cambridge, to visit with "Dr. Bernays" in order to conduct an oral history interview. I left my phone number, and indicated that, should I not hear back from him shortly, I would call again. Two days later, I received a phone call at home from Edward Bernays.

It felt weird, like a dream. Given my experience tracking his historical footprints, it was like talking-via dixie cups and a string-with a piece of history. His voice was soft, a bit hoarse, the voice of an elderly man, to be sure, but he also sounded deft and business-like.

He asked me about myself, my background, where I taught, about the book I was writing. I told him that I was a cultural historian, with a particular interest in the ways that the mass media have crisscrossed with the experiences of twentieth century American life. I told him that I knew a great deal about him, his life and contributions, and added that I had recently published a book exploring the influence of commercial imagery on the contours of American society. Without missing a beat Edward Bernays retorted, scrappily, "Of course, you know, we don't deal in images....We deal in reality."

My fascinating encounter with Edward L. Bernays had begun. I had already been offered a lesson from the master. Ideally, the job of public relations is not simply one of disseminating favorable images and impressions for a client. For Bernays and, as I would learn, for many others in the field, the goal was far more ambitious than that. Public relations was about fashioning and projecting credible renditions of reality itself.

Rather than pursue the interview by telephone—I wanted to meet him, face-to-face—I arranged to visit Edward Bernays at his home, on Columbus Day of 1990. In the weeks preceding our scheduled meeting, I re-familiarized myself with some of his writings, including *Crystallizing Public Opinion* (1923); *Propaganda* (1928); "The Engineering of Consent" (1947); and his 1965 autobiography, *Biography of an Idea: Memoirs of Public Relations* Counsel Edward L. Bernays.

Bernays, meanwhile, sought to put his own spin on the forthcoming interview. He sent me a photocopy of a biographical piece about him that had appeared recently in a special issue of *LIFE* magazine, listing the 100 most influential Americans of the twentieth century.

• • •

On the chill, gray morning of October 12, 1990, I took the shuttle from LaGuardia to Logan Airport in Boston, leaving myself enough time to arrive at Bernays' home for our scheduled one o'clock interview. Crossing the Charles River into Cambridge, the cab took me toward a maze of old, tree-lined streets bordering Harvard Square, stopping by the large red number "7" that Bernays had informed me marked his house. The house itself was stately, a large white wood-frame, surrounded by some hedges, unpretentious. Walking up the path to the door, I did not know what to expect.

I rang the doorbell and waited for an answer. A minute or two passed, and there was none. Not a sound. Had he forgotten? Was the apparent wit with which he had spoken to me on the phone only illusory? I rang again, and waited. Then, after another minute or so had passed and I had begun to grow disconsolate, I heard soft footsteps moving slowly toward the door. "Bernays?" I thought. Instead, a Chinese woman, of middle age, opened the door a crack and said, "Yes?" I told her who I was; that I had, a couple of weeks before, scheduled an interview for this afternoon with Mr. Bernays.

She looked at me quizzically, and then muttered some-thing about his having been ill yesterday. Inviting me into the house, and directing me to wait in the first floor library, she disappeared to inquire whether he was up to seeing me.

As I waited, I inspected the shelves of the spacious, high-ceilinged room in which I stood. It was a remarkable collection of books, thousands of them: about public opinion, individual and social psychology, survey research, propaganda, psycho-logical warfare, and so forth; a comprehensive library span-ning matters of human motivation and strategies of influence, scanning a period of more than one hundred years. These were not the bookshelves of some shallow huckster, but the arsenal of an intellectual. The cross hairs of nearly every volume were trained on the target of forging public attitudes. Here—in a large white room in Cambridge, Massachusetts—was the constellation of ideas that had inspired and informed a twen-tieth century preoccupation: the systematic molding of public opinion.

Captured in thought, I suddenly heard steps moving swiftly toward the library door. As the door swung open, there—standing before me in a comfy-looking brown, three-piece suit and tie, and transmitting a sparkle through his wizened eyes—was a puckish little man with thin, shaggy white hair. The swift steps I'd heard were those of Edward L. Bernays, moving toward the threshold of his one-hundredth year.

Despite years of pondering him as a shrewd and cynical manipulator of public consciousness, I was immediately entranced. His physical countenance reminded me of pictures I had seen of an aged Albert Einstein. He moved toward me and, with smiles, we exchanged formal introductions. "I want you to have this," I said, and handed him an inscribed copy of my most recent book, *All Consuming Images*, which he accepted with a nod. He then instructed me that we should go upstairs, to his office, for the interview.

He led me to the bottom of a tall staircase. On the left side there was a chair-elevator, the kind one associates with wealthy invalids in the movies. "You ever ride on one of these things?" he asked me.

"No, I've only seen them in pictures," I responded frankly.

"Get on!" he commanded me, like an elfin carny beside an amusement park ride.

I turned around and sat down, my feet resting on a metal platform at the base of the chair. "Move your feet," he ordered.

"What?"

"Move your feet back."

Without understanding I drew my feet to the back of the platform, leaving a narrow ledge in front of them. Suddenly, he stepped onto the ledge, his small pear-shaped body hovering over mine. "Should I hold you?" I asked, concerned for his frail bones.

"No," he responded dismissively, as he pushed a button on the side of the chair, and we glided up together and, turning a slight corner toward the end of the voyage, arrived on the second story. At the summit of the climb, Bernays hopped off onto the landing, and I—somewhat shakily—proceeded off behind him. "We don't deal with images," I thought, "we deal in reality."

He led me through a dark room off the landing. Its walls were covered with scores of framed black and white photographs, many of them inscribed. Wordlessly, yet eloquently, the pictures placed my ancient host close to the heartbeat of the twentieth century. Bernays on his way to the Paris Peace Conference, 1918. Bernays standing with Enrico Caruso. Bernays and Henry Ford. Bernays and Thomas Edison. Bernays

STUART EWEN

and Dwight David Eisenhower. A photo portrait of his uncle, Freud, was also conspicuous. Bernays with the "great men," at the "great events" of the twentieth century. I looked ...awestruck. He said nothing. In silence, I was fascinated, absorbed by it all.

From the photo gallery, we stepped into his small office, a solarium, and took seats by a cluttered desk. We began to talk. He began by asking me questions: about myself, my background, what had attracted me to his work in particular, and—more generally—to the broader study of communications in twentieth century America.

I opened with a rhetorical response. "How can you deal with 20th century culture without dealing with...?"

"...the basis of the exchange of ideas that makes the culture," he completed my thought.

Coming from very different vantage points, from different epochs, we understood each other. He knew what I was looking for. Within my historical study of public relations, I sought to make sense of the peculiar processes of representation and perception—the "exchange of ideas," as he put it—that have come to distinguish cultural life in the era of mass communication. Both of us, though from different vantage points, were interested in the relationship between systems of communication and the exercise of power.

• • •

The next four hours were vintage Edward Bernays. Again and again I heard word-for-word reiterations of themes, stories, even specific catch phrases that I had encountered many times before in his writings.

Nonetheless, beyond the actual experience of meeting with Bernays, some parts of the interview were new to me.

I was particularly intrigued, for example, by Bernays' reflections on the connection between his own thinking and that of Walter Lippmann. While *Crystallizing Public Opinion* contains many ideas derived from Lippmann, he believed that his own book was more practical, less academic.

> Lippmann treated public opinion on a purely theoretical basis. He never got down to matters of changing it. He talks of it as if he were a sociologist dis-cussing a social caste system…abstractly. And I was surprised. Here he was, a working newspaperman.

Another interesting point in our conversation came when he spoke of his wife, and business partner, Doris E. Fleischman. The two had worked as a team from 1922, when they were married, until her death in 1980. Though Fleischman was a lifelong feminist, and continued to use her own name—even after marriage—her identity within Bernays's public relations firm was furtive.

As Bernays put it to me, "If I'm speaking with Alfred P. Sloan, Chairman of the Board of General Motors, he doesn't want to know that his company's approach to the public was designed by a woman."

"So how was she known?" I inquired.

His response: "She was known as Edward L. Bernays."

• • •

There were, however, some other aspects of the interview that are worth recounting here, aspects that reflect on the history and meaning of public relations itself.

Throughout the interview Bernays expressed an unabashedly

hierarchical view of society. Repeatedly, he maintained that, while most people respond to their world instinctively, without thought, there exist an "intelligent few" who have been charged with the responsibility of contemplating and influencing the tide of history. Perceived by Bernays as one of these "few," he was willing to share his outlook with me in straightforward terms.

Although he had written extensively, over a lifetime, about democracy and on the important role that public relations plays in a democratic society, Bernays, himself, was clearly no democrat. He expressed little respect for the average person's ability to think out, understand, or act upon the world in which they live.

"There are strange things about the culture," he intoned. "The average IQ is 100 of the American public, did you know that?" Assuming I grasped what for him was obvious, Bernays then sketched a picture of the public relations expert as a member of the "intelligent few" who advises clients on how to "deal with the masses...just by applying psychology."

As a member of that intellectual elite which guides the destiny of society, the PR "professional," Bernays explained, aims his craft at a general public that is essentially, and unreflectively, reactive. Working behind the scenes, out of public view, the public relations expert is "an applied social scientist," one educated to employ an understanding of "sociology, psychology, social psychology and economics" in order to influence and direct public attitudes. This notion was expressed succinctly in Bernays's 1928 book, *Propaganda*.

> Trotter and Le Bon concluded that the group mind does not think in the strict sense of the word. In place of thought it has impulses, habits and emotions. In making up its mind, its first impulse is usually to

follow the example of a trusted leader. This is one of the most firmly established principles of mass psychology.

Throughout our conversation, Bernays conveyed his hallucination of democracy, where a highly educated class of opinion-molding tacticians are continuously at work, analyzing the social terrain and adjusting the mental scenery from which the public mind, with its limited intellect, derives its opinions.

Undoubtedly, this point of view offers a glimpse into Edward L. Bernays. More importantly, it reflects a foundational conceit governing the field of public relations more broadly. While some have argued that public relations represents a "two-way street" through which institutions and the public carry on a democratic dialog, the public's role within that alleged dialog is, most often, one of having its blood pressure monitored, its temperature taken.

$$\cdots$$

Another phase of the interview deserves special mention. I came to visit Bernays because he was both a participant in, and a witness to, the rise of public relations over a period of nearly three-quarters of a century. Anticipating the interview, I hoped that his recollections would provide me with some new and clear sense of the particular historical soil out of which public relations, as a phenomenon, grew. In this regard I was, for the most part, frustrated. As I prepared to depart from him, I felt a bit disappointed in this regard.

Then, as we began discussing the means by which I would get from his house back to the airport, a curious conversation unfolded. Amid a general complaint about the cost of taxicabs, and after counseling me to save my money and hop a trolley, Edward Bernays indicated that he, himself, had never learned how to drive an automobile. I expressed surprise. He explained that he had simply never had to learn to drive; among his family's staff of up to thirteen servants, there was always a chauffeur.

Bernays then proceeded to tell me the story of one chauffeur in particular, a man he called "Dumb Jack."

Each day, he related to me, Dumb Jack would awaken at 5 o'clock in the morning, and prepare to drive Bernays and his wife (and partner in public relations), Doris Fleishman, to the office. The trusty chauffeur would then return to the family home to carry their two daughters to school. From there, he would return to the office in order to chauffeur Bernays and his wife to business meetings through¬out the day, taking time out to retrieve the daughters from their school. At the end of the day, according to Bernays, a subdued Dumb Jack would step into the kitchen and, as the cook prepared the evening meal, he would sit at a kitchen table, lay his head in his hands, and take a nap. He would go to bed at nine, only to begin his routine again the next morning at five. Comparing this situation favorably to the cost of one cab ride to the airport today, Bernays ended his story by saying that for all of this work, Dumb Jack received a salary of twenty-five dollars per week, and got a half a Thursday off every two weeks.

"Not a bad deal," Bernays confided, characterizing the benefits that his family had derived from Dumb Jack's years of compliant service. Then, with a lilt of nostalgia in his voice, he concluded his story: "But that's before people got a social conscience."

At that moment, in that nostalgic reverie over a bygone era, my quest for historical explanation—or at least a piece of it—was satisfied. In an incidental reference to "social conscience,"

Bernays had illuminated an historic shift in the social history of property, shedding inadvertent light on the conditions that gave birth to the birth of the practice of public relations. As the twentieth century progressed, people were no longer willing to accommodate themselves to outmoded standards of deference which history, for millennia, had demanded of them.

Bernays was the child of an haute bourgeois world that was, in many ways, still captivated by aristocratic styles of wealth, where relations between the classes were marked, to a large extent, by deep-seated patterns of allegiance of obedience and obligation between masters and servants. Dumb Jack was a child of these circumstances.

The "social conscience," to which Bernays referred, arrived at that moment when aristocratic paradigms of deference could no longer hold up in the face of modern, democratic, public ideals that were boiling up among the "lower strata" of society. At that juncture, strategies of social rule began to change, and the life and career of Edward Bernays, I should add, serves as a testament to that change.

The explosive ideals of democracy challenged ancient customs that had long upheld social inequality. A public claiming the birthright of democratic citizenship and social justice increasingly called upon institutions and people of power to justify themselves and their privileges. In the crucible of these changes, aristocracy began to give way to technocracy as a strategy of rule. Bernays came to maturity in a society where the exigencies of power were—by necessity—increasingly exercised from behind the pretext of the "common good."

Bernays, the child of aristocratic pretense who fashioned himself into a technician of mass persuasion, was the product of a "social conscience" that had grasped the fact that once-submissive "Dumb Jacks," in the contemporary world, would no longer be willing to quietly place his tired head in his folded hands at the end of each day, only to awaken and serve again the next morning. Born into privilege, developing into a technocrat, Bernays' biography illustrates the onus that the twentieth century had placed on social and economic elites; they have had to justify themselves continually to a public whose hearts and minds now bear the ideals of democracy.

As I pursued my research on public relations, following my encounter with Bernays, and repeatedly ran into the fear of an empowered public that ignited the thinking of early practitioners of public relations, the story of "Dumb Jack"—the man who was no more—came to mind again and again, reminding me of the human flesh that encircles the bones of broad institutional developments.

• • •

Another story bears repeating here. Towards the middle of our interview, hoping that I could gain insight into the way Bernays approached his practical work, I asked him to describe how he would plan and attend to a specific public relations assignment. First of all, Bernays instructed, one must rid one's mind of the conventional "press agent" image. "We've [speaking of himself] had no direct contact with the mass media for about fifty years." Rather, he continued, the job of a public relations counsel is to instruct a client on how to take actions that "just interrupt...the continuity of life in some way to bring about the [media] response."

"How would you do that?" I asked.

Bernays thought for a moment, and then turned toward his desk, where he had earlier placed the copy of my book. He picked it up and began to fondle its cover between his small, pinkish-gray fingers; glancing down at the front of the book, reading, to himself, the descriptive material and blurbs that appeared on its back. Then, with a tone of momentousness in his voice, he turned to me:

> If you said to me, 'I would like more readers of this book [tapping the cover] ...I would immediately get in touch with the largest American consumer association. And I would say to the head of the consumers association, 'There are undoubtedly...I can't tell you the exact percentage, but X percentage of your members who are very definitely interested in the images that come from a finance capitalist society, and who I think would enjoy hearing about that. Why don't you devote one of your twelve meetings a year to consumer images, the name of a new book, and I think it may be possible for me to get the author to talk to the New York meeting and you then make an arrangement with American Tel and Tel and have a video tape made of him beforehand and in thirty of the largest cities of the United States that have the American Consumer League, you listen to an in-depth concept of consumers and images....

Then Bernays turned to me and, with an abracadabra tone in his voice, he summarized the imaginable result of his hypothetical phone-call to the head of the country's largest consumer association:

> Every one of the consumer groups has contacts with the local paper, and in some cases the AP may pick it

up, or Reuters, and you become an international star!

I must acknowledge that I was thoroughly charmed. Here I was, sitting with Edward Bernays—innovator and artiste of modern public relations—listening to him apply his costly wizardry to me and my book. I couldn't get over it, and thought to myself, "What a flatterer. This guy really knows how to polish up the old apple." For weeks after the interview, I was tickled by the incident, retelling it to friends, students, whoever had the patience to listen. For me the story captured Bernays's engaging personality, his ingenious thought process, his ability to garner a response. With time it also reminded me of the chilling fact that charm and deception too often go hand in glove.

Then, about three months after the interview—the above incident having faded from my immediate memory—I received a most surprising telephone call. It was from Steven Brobeck, president of the Consumer Federation of America, one of the nation's largest and most influential consumer organizations. Mr. Brobeck wanted to know if I would be willing to serve as a keynote speaker at the upcoming Consumer Congress in Washington, DC, a convention that would bring together more than a thousand members of consumer organizations from around the country. He wanted me to speak about American consumer culture and the ways that seductive commercial images are routinely employed to promote waste and disposability. C-Span, I was informed, would be taping my key-note, and would then cablecast it across the country.

I still do not know whether Bernays' hand was behind this invitation, or whether the phone call was merely a result of sly coincidence. When I inquired as to the origin of the invitation, nowhere was there any clear-cut, or even circumstantial, evidence of Bernays's intervention.

But then I recalled another point in our lengthy conversation, when Bernays sermonized on the invisibility with which public relations experts must, ideally, perform their handiwork.

When I noted that, even though *LIFE* magazine had included him in the list of the one hundred most influential Americans in the twentieth century, most Americans would probably not know who he was, he responded:

> I'm sure of it.... To the average American your name has to be Walter Cronkite, or...[you have to be] the most beautiful girl... some movie actress they know.... In public relations, just as in law, you don't—nobody knows—who the lawyer of most people is, and that lawyer may do more than the brain of the man who is theoretically doing it.... And I think it should be that way because nobody knows who my doctor is. I mean, except friends. And he may be the basis of my living.

And there I was; the mystery still unsolved. Yet the question remained, and remains, open. Things had uncannily come to pass much as Bernays had described in his hypothetical disquisition on the work of a PR practitioner, and one was left to ponder whether there is any reality anymore, save the reality of public relations?

One last point. I had gone to Cambridge to interview Edward Bernays and gather details from the master regarding the history of the hidden—yet omnipresent—activities of public relations. In retrospect, I had greatly underestimated the individual with whom I would be talking. I had presupposed that this keenly aware shaper of public perception, this trader in realities, was at the same time open to being candidly cross-examined. Yet in the days following our meeting, it became clear to me that my entire visit had been orchestrated by a virtuoso.

He had even offered me the key by which the pageantry of our encounter might have been unlocked. During the extensive taped interview that I assumed I was conducting, Bernays had at one point turned to me, and announced:

> News is any overt act which juts out of the routine of circumstance. ...A good public relations man advises his client...to carry out an overt act... interrupting the continuity of life in some way to bring about a response.

From the time I had approached the door of his house, waiting impatiently for an answer; to my ride on the staircase elevator; to my walk through the gallery of historical photographs, on to the time, five hours later, when we parted company, Edward Bernays—who still claimed to charge $1,000 per hour consulting fees—was giving me—free of charge, an empirical object lesson in public relations.

In 1995, Bernays died at the age of 103. Since his death, interest in his life and work has only grown. The book that follows, *Crystallizing Public Opinion*, offers the most comprehensive account of the ideas that influenced him, and provides a crystal clear presentation of the strategic approaches that made up the modern field of public relations at the moment of its inception, approaches that still endure. If anything, the twenty-first century has witnessed the encroachment of Bernays's ideas into every crevice of our lives.

Stuart Ewen
Truro, Massachusetts
May 2011

ENDNOTES

1. The phrase "invisible wirepuller" was Bernays's own, a self-description found in his 1928 book, *Propaganda*, p. 60.

2. John Stauber and Sheldon Rampton's 1995 book about public relations, *Toxic Sludge Is Good For You*, continues to inform a large number of readers about Bernays's influence. Larry Tye's *The Father of Spin: Edward L. Bernays and the Birth of Public Relations*, (New York: Crown 1998), has also helped to spread Bernays's posthumous reputation.

A 2002 film produced by the Media Education Foundation, also entitled "Toxic Sludge is Good For You," brought repeated mention of Bernays's work into a wide range of American high school and college classrooms. Noam Chomsky, in his short book *Media Control: The Spectacular Achievements of Propaganda*, (New York: Open Media 2002), has also highlighted Bernays's work.

My own books have also familiarized many people with Bernays. Initially, I discussed him in *Captains of Consciousness: Advertising and the Social Roots of the Consumer Culture* (New York: McGraw-Hill, 1976). A much fuller and more informed presentation of Edward Bernays and his social impact is found in my 1996 book, *PR! A Social History of Spin*, (New York: Basic Books).

Unexpectedly PR! provided a foundation for Adam Curtis's four-part award winning documentary film series, "The

Century of the Self," which includes an hour-long segment focusing on Bernays. Initially seen on BBC television, and screened theatrically in New York Curtis's powerful series has assumed a cult status and has, probably more than any other source, provided a growing circle of people with a vivid picture of Bernays's influence on twentieth and twenty-first century society. All four parts are available for viewing on the internet.

Long out of print, Ig Publishing's project to make Bernay's books available again, beginning with *Propaganda* (1928), with an excellent introduction by Mark Crispin Miller, and continuing with this volume, is only likely to enhance greater public awareness of Bernays and his impact on everyday life in the United States and elsewhere.

3. See Stephen Schlesinger, Stephen Kinzer, John H. Coatsworth and Richard A. Nuccio, *Bitter Fruit: The Story of an American Coup in Guatamala*, (Cambridge: Harvard University Press, 1999). See also, Larry Tye, op cit, pp. 160-182. Bernays mentions his involvement in his autobiography, *Biography of an Idea: Memoirs of a Public Relations Counsel*, (New York: Simon and Schuster, 1995).

4. Robert Cialdini coined the term "compliance professionals" in *Influence: The New Psychology of Modern Persuasion*, (New York: Harper, 1984).

5.Edward Bernays, *Propaganda*, (Ig Publishing: Brooklyn, 2005). Originally published 1928.

CRYSTALLIZING PUBLIC OPINION

FOREWORD

In writing this book I have tried to set down the board principles that govern the new profession of public relations counsel. These principles I have on the one hand substantiated by the findings of psychologists, sociologists, and newspapermen—Ray Stannard Baker, W.G. Bleyer, Richard Washburn Child, Elmer Davis, John L. Given, Will Irwin, Francis E. Leupp, Walter Lippmann, William MacDougall, Everett Dean Martin, H.L. Mencken, Rollo Ogden, Charles J. Rosebault, William Trotter, Oswald Garrison Villard, and others to whom I owe a debt of gratitude for their clear analyses of the public's mind and habits; and on the other hand, I have illustrated these principles by a number of specific examples which serve to bear them out. I have quoted from the men listed here, because the ground covered by them is part of the field of activity of the public relations counsel. The actual cases which I have cited were selected because they explain the application of the theories to practice. Most of the illustrative material is drawn from my personal experience; a few examples from my observation of events. I have preferred to cite facts known to the general public, in order that I might explain graphically a profession that has little precedent, and whose few formulated rules have necessarily a limitless number and variety of applications.

This profession in a few years has developed from the status of circus agent stunts to what is obviously an important position in the conduct of the world's affairs.

If I shall, by this survey of the field, stimulate a scientific attitude towards the study of public relations, I shall feel that this book has fulfilled my purpose in writing it.

E.L.B.

PART I

SCOPE AND FUNCTIONS

CHAPTER I

THE SCOPE OF THE PUBLIC
RELATIONS COUNSEL

A new phrase has come into the language—counsel on public relations. What does it mean?

As a matter of fact, the actual phrase is completely understood by only a few, and those only the people intimately associated with the work itself. But despite this, the activities of the public relations counsel affect the daily life of the entire population in one form or another.

Because of the recent extraordinary growth of the profession of public relations counsel and the lack of available information concerning it, an air of mystery has surrounded its scope and functions. To the average person, this profession is still unexplained, both in its operation and actual accomplishment. Perhaps the most definite picture is that of a man who somehow or other produces that vaguely defined evil, "propaganda," which spreads an impression that colors the mind of the public concerning actresses, governments, railroads. And yet, as will be pointed out shortly, there is probably no single profession which within the last ten years has extended its field of usefulness more remarkably and touched upon intimate and important aspects of the everyday life of the world more significantly than the profession of public relations counsel.

There is not event any one name by which the new profession is characterized by others. To some the public relations
counsel is known by the term "propagandist." Others still call
him press agent or publicity man. Writing even within the last
few years, John L. Given, the author of an excellent textbook
on journalism, does not mention the public relations counsel.
He limits his reference to the old-time press agent. Many organizations simply do not bother about an individual name or
assign to an existing officer the duties of the public relations
counsel. One bank's vice-president is its recognized public
relations counsel. Some dismiss the subject or condemn the
entire profession generally and all its members individually.

Slight examination into the grounds for this disapproval
readily reveals that it is based on nothing more substantial
than vague impressions.

Indeed, it is probably true that the very men who are
themselves engaged in the profession are as little ready or able
to define their work as is the general public itself. Undoubtedly this is due, in some measure, to the fact that the profession is a new one. Much more important than that, however,
is the fact that most human activities are based on experience
rather than analysis.

Judge Cardozo of the Court of Appeals of the State of
New York finds the same absence of functional definition in
the judicial mind. "The work of deciding cases," he says, "goes
on every day in hundreds of courts throughout the land. Any
judge, one might suppose, would find it easy to describe the
process which he had followed a thousand times and more.
Nothing could be further from the truth. Let some intelligent
layman ask him to explain. He will not go very far before
taking refuge in the excuse that the language of craftsmen is
unintelligible to those untutored in the craft. Such an excuse

may cover with a semblance of respectability an otherwise ignominious retreat. It will hardly serve to still the prick of curiosity and conscience. In moments of introspection, when there is no longer a necessity of putting off with a show of wisdom the uninitiated interlocutor, the troublesome problem will recur and press for a solution: What is it that I do when I decide a case?"

From my own records and from current history still fresh in the public mind, I have selected a few instances which only in a limited measure give some idea of the variety of the public relations counsel's work and of the type of problem which he attempts to solve.

These examples show him in his position as one who directs and supervises the activities of his clients wherever they impinge upon the daily life of the public. He interprets the client to the public, which he is enabled to do in part because he interprets the public to the client. His advice is given on all occasions on which his client appears before the public, whether it be in concrete form or as an idea. His advice is given not only on actions which take place, but also on the use of mediums which bring these actions to the public it is desired to reach, no matter whether these mediums be the printed, the spoken or the visualized word—that is, advertising, lectures, the stage, the pulpit, the newspaper, the photograph, the wireless, the mail or any other form of thought communication.

A nationally famous New York hotel found that its business was falling off at an alarming rate because of a rumor that it was shortly going to close and that the site upon which it was located would be occupied by a department store. Few things are more mysterious than the origins of rumors, or the credence which they manage to obtain. Reservations at this hotel for weeks and months ahead were being canceled by persons who had heard the rumor and accepted it implicitly.

The problem of meeting this rumor (which like many rumors had no foundation in fact) was not only a difficult but a serious one. Mere denial, of course, no matter how vigorous or how widely disseminated, would accomplish little.

The mere statement of the problem made it clear to the public relations counsel who was retained by the hotel that the only way to overcome the rumor was to give the public some positive evidence of the intention of the hotel to remain in business. It happened that the *maitre d'hotel* was about as well known as the hotel itself. His contract was about to expire. The public relations counsel suggested a very simple device.

"Renew his engagement immediately for a term of years," he said. "Then make public announcement of the fact. Nobody who hears of the renewal or the amount of money involved will believe for a moment that you intend to go out of business." The *maitre d'hotel* was called in and offered a five-year engagement. His salary was one which many bank presidents might envy. Public announcement of his engagement was made. The *maitre d'hotel* was himself something of a national figure. The salary stipulated was not without popular interest from both points of view. The story was one which immediately interested the newspapers. A national press service took up the story and sent it out to all its subscribers. The cancellation of reservations stopped and the rumor disappeared.

A nationally known magazine was ambitious to increase its prestige among a more influential group of advertisers. It had never made any effort to reach this public except through its own direct circulation. The consultant who was retained by the magazine quickly discovered that much valuable editorial material appearing in the magazine was allowed to go to waste. Features of interest to thousands of potential readers were never called to their attention unless they happened accidentally to be readers of the magazine.

The public relations counsel showed how to extend the field of their appeal. He chose for his first work an extremely interesting article by a well-known physician, written about the interesting thesis that "the pace that kills" is the slow, deadly dull routine pace and not the pace of life under high pressure, based on work which interests and excites. The consultant arranged to have the thesis of the article made the basis of an inquiry among business and professional men throughout the country by another physician associated with a medical journal. Hundreds of members of "the quality public," as they are known to advertisers, had their attention focused on the article, and the magazine which the consultant was engaged in counseling on its public relations.

The answers from these leading men of the country were collated, analyzed, and the resulting abstract furnished gratuitously to newspapers, magazines and class journals, which published them widely. Organizations of business and professional men reprinted the symposium by the thousands and distributed it free of charge, doing so because the material contained in the symposium was of great interest. A distinguished visitor from abroad, Lord Leverhulme, became interested in the question while in this country and made the magazine and the article the basis of an address before a large and influential conference in England. Nationally and internationally the magazine was called to the attention of a public which had, up to that time, considered it perhaps a publication of no serious social significance.

Still working with the same magazine, the publicity consultant advised it how to widen its influence with another public on quite a different issue. He took as his subject an article by Sir Philip Gibbs, "The Madonna of the Hungry Child," dealing with the famine situation in Europe and the necessity for its prompt alleviation. The article was brought to the attention of Herbert Hoover. Mr. Hoover was so impressed by the article that he sent the magazine a letter of commendation for publishing it. He also sent a copy of the article to members of his relief committees throughout the country. The latter, in turn, used the article to obtain support and contributions for relief work. Thus, while an important humanitarian project was being materially assisted, the magazine in question was adding to its own influence and standing.

Now, the interesting thing about this work is that whereas the public relations counsel added nothing to the contents of the magazine, which had for years been publishing material of this nature, he did make its importance felt and appreciated.

A large packing house was faced with the problem of increasing the sale of its particular brand of bacon. It already dominated the market in its field; the problem was therefore one of increasing the consumption of bacon generally, for its dominance of the market would naturally continue. The public relations counsel, realizing that hearty breakfasts were dietetically sound, suggested that a physician undertake a survey to make this medical truth articulate. He realized that the demand for bacon as a breakfast food would naturally be increased by the wide dissemination of this truth. This is exactly what happened.

A hair-net company had to solve the problem created by the increasing vogue of bobbed hair. Bobbed hair was eliminating the use of the hair-net. The public relations counsel, after investigation, advised that the opinions of club women as leaders of the women of the country should be made articulate on the question. Their expressed opinion, he believed, would definitely modify the bobbed hair vogue. A leading artist was interested in the subject and undertook a survey among the club women leaders of the country. The resultant responses confirmed the public relations counsel's judgment. The opinions of these women were given to the public and helped to arouse what had evidently been a latent opinion on the question. Long hair was made socially more acceptable than bobbed hair and the vogue for the latter was thereby partially checked.

A real estate corporation on Long Island was interested in selling cooperative apartments to a high-class clientele. In order to do this, it realized that it had to impress upon the public the fact that this community, within easy reach of Manhattan, was socially, economically, artistically and morally desirable. On the advice of its public relations counsel, instead of merely proclaiming itself as such a community, it proved its contentions dramatically by making itself an active center for all kinds of community manifestations.

When it opened its first post office, for instance, it made this local event nationally interesting. The opening was a formal one. National figures became interested in what might have been merely a local event.

The reverses which the Italians suffered on the Piave in 1918 were dangerous to Italian and Allied morale. One of the results was the awakening of a distrust among Italians as to the sincerely of American promises of military, financial and moral support for the Italian cause.

It became imperative vividly to dramatize for Italy the reality of American cooperation. As one of the means to this end the Committee on Public Relations Information decided that the naming of a recently completed American ship should be made the occasion for a demonstration of friendship which could be reflected in every possible way to the Italians.

Prominent Italians in America were invited by the public relations counsel to participate in the launching of the *Piave*. Motion and still pictures were taken of the event. The news of the launching and its significance to Americans was telegraphed to Italian newspapers. At the same time a message from Italian-Americans was transmitted to Italy expressing their confidence in America's assistance of the Italian cause. Enrico Caruso, Gatti-Casazza, director of the Metropolitan Opera, and others highly regarded by their countrymen in Italy, sent inspiriting telegrams which had a decided effect in raising Italian morale, so far as it depended upon the assurance of American cooperation. Other means employed to disseminate information of this event had the same effect.

The next incident that I have selected is one which conforms more closely than some of the others to the popular conception of the work of the public relations counsel. In the spring and summer of 1919 the problem of fitting ex-service men into the ordinary life of America was serious and difficult. Thousands of men just back from abroad were having a trying time finding work. After their experience in the war it was not surprising that they should be extremely ready to feel bitter against the Government and against those Americans who for one reason or another had not been in any branch of the service during the war.

The War Department under Colonel Arthur Woods, assistant to the Secretary of War, instituted a nation-wide campaign to assist those men to obtain employment, and more than that, to manifest to them as concretely as it could that the Government continued its interest in their welfare. The incident to which I refer occurred during this campaign.

In July of 1919 there was such a shortage of labor in Kansas that it was feared a large proportion of the wheat crop could not possibly be harvested. The activities of the War Department in the reemployment of ex-service men had already received wide publicity, and the Chamber of Commerce of Kansas City appealed directly to the War Department at Washington, after its own efforts in many other directions had failed, for a supply of men who would assist in the harvesting of the wheat crop. The public relations counsel prepared a statement of this opportunity for employment in Kansas and distributed it to the public through the newspapers throughout the country. The Associated Press sent the statement over its wires as a news dispatch. Within four days the Kansas City Chamber of Commerce wired to the War Department that enough labor had been secured to harvest the wheat crop, and asked the War Department to announce that fact as publicly as it had first announced the need for labor.

By contrast with this last instance, and as an illustration of a type of work less well understood by the public, I cite another incident from the same campaign for the reestablishment of ex-service men to normal economic and social relations. The problem of reemployment was, of course, the crux of the difficulty. Various measures were adopted to obtain the cooperation of business men in extending employment opportunities to ex-members of the Army, Navy and Marines. One of these devices appealed to the personal and local pride of American businessmen, and stressed their obligation of honor to reemploy their former employees upon release from Government service.

A citation was prepared, signed by the Secretary of War, the Secretary of the Navy and the Assistant to the Secretary of War for display in the stores and factories of employers who assured the War and Navy Departments that they would reemploy their ex-service men. Simultaneous display of these citations was arranged for Bastille Day, July 14, 1919, by members of the Fifth Avenue Association.

The Fifth Avenue Association of New York City, an influential group of business men, was perhaps the first to cooperate as a body in this important campaign for the reemployment of ex-service men. Concerted action on a subject which was as much in the public mind as the reemployment of ex-service men was particularly interesting. The story of what these leaders in American business had undertaken to do went out to the country by mail, by word of mouth, by newspaper comment. Their example was potent in obtaining the cooperation of business men thoroughout the land. An appeal based on this action and capitalizing it was sent to thousands of individual business men and employers throughout the country. It was effective.

An illustration which embodies most of the technical and psychological points of interest in the preceding incidents may be found in Lithuania's campaign in this country in 1919, for popular sympathy and official recognition. Lithuania was of considerable political importance in the reorganization of Europe, but it was a country little known or understood by the American public. An added difficulty was the fact that the independence of Lithuania would interfere seriously with the plans which France had for the establishment of a strong Poland. There were excellent historical, ethnic and economic reasons why, if Lithuania broke off from Russia, it should be allowed to stand on its own feet. On the other hand there were powerful political influences which were against such a result. The American attitude on the question of Lithuanian independence, it was felt, would play an important part. The question was how to arouse popular and official interest in Lithuania's aspirations.

A Lithuanian National Council was organized, composed of prominent American-Lithuanians, and a Lithuanian Information Bureau established to act as a clearing house for news about Lithuania and for special pleading on behalf of Lithuania's ambitions. The public relations counsel who was retained to direct this work recognized that the first problem to be solved was America's indifference to and ignorance about Lithuania and its desires.

He had an exhaustive study made of every conceivable aspect of the problem of Lithuania from its remote and recent history and ethnic origins to its present-day marriage customs and its popular recreations. He divided his material into its various categories, based primarily on the public to which it would probably make its appeal. For the amateur ethnologist he provided interesting and accurate data of the racial origins of Lithuania. To the student of languages he appealed with authentic and well written studies of the development of the Lithuanian language from its origins in the Sanskrit. He told the "sporting fan" about Lithuanian sports and told American women about Lithuanian clothes. He told the jeweler about amber and provided the music lover with concerts of Lithuanian music.

To the senators, he gave facts about Lithuania which would give them basis for favorable action. To the members of the House of Representatives he did likewise. He reflected to those communities whose crystallized opinion would be helpful in guiding other opinions, facts which gave them basis for conclusions favorable to Lithuania.

A series of events which would carry with them the desired implications were planned and executed. Mass meetings were held in different cities; petitions were drawn, signed and presented; pilgrims made calls upon Senate and House of Representatives Committees. All the avenues of approach to the public were utilized to capitalize the public interest and bring public action. The mails carried statements of Lithuania's position to individuals who might be interested. The lecture platform resounded to Lithuania's appeal. Newspaper advertising was bought and paid for. The radio carried the message of speakers to the public. Motion pictures reached the patrons of moving picture houses.

Little by little and phase by phase, the public, the press and Government officials acquired a knowledge of the customs, the character and the problems of Lithuania, the small Baltic nation that was seeking freedom.

When the Lithuanian Information Bureau went before the press associations to correct inaccurate or misleading Polish news about the Lithuanian situation, it came there as representative of a group which had figured largely in the American news for a number of weeks, as a result of the advice and activities of its public relations counsel. In the same way, when delegations of Americans, interested in the Lithuanian problem, appeared before members of Congress or officials of the State Department, they came there as spokesmen for country which was no longer unknown. They represented a group which could no longer be entirely ignored. Somebody described this campaign, once it had achieved recognition for the Baltic republic, as the campaign of "advertising a nation to freedom."

What happened with Romania is another instance. Romania wanted to plead its case before the American people. It wanted to tell Americans that it was an ancient and established country. The original technique was the issuance of treatises, historically correct and ethnologically accurate. Their facts were for the large part ignored. The public relations counsel, called in on the case of Romania, advised them to make these studies into interesting stories of news value. The public read these stories with avidity and Romania became part of America's popular knowledge with consequent valuable results for Romania.

The hotels in New York City discovered that there was a falling off of business and profits. Fewer visitors came to New York. Fewer travelers passed through New York on their way to Europe. The public relations counsel who was consulted and asked to remedy the situation, made an extensive analysis. He talked to visitors. He queried men and women who represented groups, sections and opinions of main cities and towns throughout the country. He examined American literature—books, magazines, newspapers, and classified attacks made on New York and New York citizens. He found that the chief cause for lack of interest in New York was the belief that New York was "cold and inhospitable."

He found animosity and bitterness against New York's apparent indifference to strangers was keeping away a growing number of travelers. To counteract this damaging wave of resentment, he called together the leading groups, industrial, social and civic, of New York and formed the Welcome Stranger Committee. The friendly and hospitable aims of this committee, broadcasted to the nation, helped to reestablish New York's good repute. Congratulatory editorials were printed in the rural and city journals of the country.

Again, in analyzing the restaurant service of a prominent hotel, he discovers that its menu is built on the desires of the average eater and that a large group of people with children desire special foods for them. He may then advise his client to institute a children's diet service.

This was done specifically with the Waldorf Astoria Hotel, which instituted special menus for children. This move, which excited wide comment, was economically and dietetically sound.

Its campaign to educate the public on the importance of early radium treatments for incipient cancer, the United States Radium Corporation founded the First National Radium Bank, in order to create and crystallize the impression that radium is and should be available to all physicians who treat cancer sufferers.

An inter-city radio company planned to open a wireless service between the three cities of New York, Detroit and Cleveland. This company might merely have opened its service and waited for the public to send its messages, but the president of the organization realized astutely that to succeed in any measure at all he must have immediate public support. He called in a public relations counsel, who advised an elaborate inauguration ceremony, in which the mayors of the three cities thus for the first time connected, would officiate. The mayor of each city officially received and sent the first messages issued on commercial inter-city radio waves. These openings excited wide interest, not only in the three cities directly concerned, but throughout the entire country.

Shortly after the World War, the King and Queen of the Belgians visited America. One of the many desired results of this visit was that it should be made apparent that America, with all the foreign elements represented in its body, was unified in its support of King Albert and his country. To present a graphic picture of the affection which the national elements here had for the Belgian monarch, a performance was staged at the Metropolitan Opera House in New York City, at which the many nationalist groups were represented and gave voice to their approval. The story of the Metropolitan Opera House performance was spread in the news columns and by photographs in the press throughout the world. It was evident to all who saw the pictures or read the story that this king had really stirred the affectionate interest of the national elements that make up America.

An interesting illustration of the broad field of work of the public relations counsel today is noted in the efforts which were exerted to secure wide commendation and support among Americans for the League of Nations. Obviously a small group of persons, banded together for the sole purpose of furthering the appeal of the League, would have no powerful effect. In order to secure a certain homogeneity among the members of groups who individually had widely varied interests and affiliations, it was decided to form a non-partisan committee for the League of Nations.

The public relations consultant, having assisted in the formation of this committee, called a meeting of women representing Democratic, Republican, radical, reactionary, club, society, professional and industrial groups, and suggested that they make a united appeal for national support of the League of Nations. This meeting accurately and dramatically reflected disinterested and unified support of the League. The public relations counsel made articulate what would otherwise have remained a strong passive element. The still inconsistent demand for the League of Nations is undoubtedly due in part to efforts of this nature.

Cases as diverse as the following are the daily work of the public relations counsel. One client is advised to give up a Rolls-Royce car and to buy a Ford, because the public has definite concepts of what ownership of each represents—another man may be given the contrary advice. One client is advised to withdraw the hat-check privilege, because it causes unfavorable public comments. Another is advised to change the facade of his building to conform to a certain public taste.

One client is advised to announce changes of price policy to the public by telegraph, another by circular, another by advertising. One client is advised to publish a Bible, another a book of French Renaissance tales.

One department store is advised to use prices in its advertising, another store not to mention them.

A client is advised to make his labor policy, the hygienic aspect of his factory, his own personality, part of his sales campaign.

Another client is advised to exhibit his wares in a museum and school.

Still another is urged to found a scholarship in his subject at a leading university.

Further incidents could be given here, illustrating different aspects of the ordinary daily functions of the public relations counsel—how, for example, the production of "Damaged Goods" in America became the basis of the first notably successful move in this country for overcoming the prudish refusal to appreciate and face the place of sex in human life; or how, more recently, the desire of some great corporations to increase their business was, through the advice of Ivy Lee, their public relations counsel, made the basis of the popular education on the importance of brass and copper to civilization. Enough has been cited, however, to show how little the average member of the public knows of the real work of the public relations counsel, and how that work impinges upon the daily life of the public in an almost infinite number of ways.

Popular misunderstanding of the work of the public relations counsel is easily comprehensible because of the short period of his development. Nevertheless, the fact remains that he has become in recent years too important a figure in American life for this ignorance to be safely or profitably continued.

CHAPTER II

THE PUBLIC RELATIONS COUNSEL;
THE INCREASED AND INCREASING
IMPORTANCE OF THE PROFESSION

The rise of the modern public relations counsel is based on the need for and the value of his services. Perhaps the most significant social, political and industrial fact about the present century is the increased attention which is paid to pubic opinion, not only by individuals, groups or movements that are dependent on public support for their success, but also by men and organizations which until very recently stood aloof from the general public and were able to say, "The public be damned."

The public today demands information and expects also to be accepted as judge and jury in matters that have a wide public import. The public, whether it invests its money in subway or railroad tickets, in hotel rooms or restaurant fare, in silk or soap, is a highly sophisticated body. It asks questions, and if the answer in word or action is not forthcoming or satisfactory, it turns to other sources for information or relief.

The willingness to spend thousands of dollars in obtaining professional advice on how best to present one's views or products to a public is based on this fact.

On every side of American life, whether political, industrial, social, religious or scientific, the increasing pressure of public judgment has made itself felt. Generally speaking, the relationship and interaction of the public and any movement is rather obvious. The charitable society which depends upon voluntary contributions for its support has a clear and direct interest in being favorably represented before the public. In the same way, the great corporation which is in danger of having its profits taxed away or its sales fall off or its freedom impeded by legislative action must have recourse to the public to combat successfully these menaces. Behind these obvious phenomena, however, lie three recent tendencies of fundamental importance; first, the tendency of small organizations to aggregate into groups of such size and importance that the public tends to regard them as semi-public services; second, the increased readiness of the public, due to the spread of literacy and democratic forms of government, to feel that it is entitled to its voice in the conduct of these large aggregations, political, capitalist or labor, or whatever they may be; third, the keen competition for public favor due to modern methods of "selling."

An example of the first tendency—that is, the tendency toward an increased public interest in industrial activity, because of the increasing social importance of industrial aggregations—may be found in an article on "The Critic and the Law" by Richard Washburn Child, published in the *Atlantic Monthly* for May, 1906.

Mr. Child discusses in that article the right of the critic to say uncomplimentary things about matters of public interest. He points out the legal basis for the right to criticize plays and novels. Then he adds, "A vastly more important and interesting theory, and one which must arise from the present state and tendency of industrial conditions, is whether the acts of men in commercial activity may ever become so prominent and so far reaching in their effect that they compel a universal public interest and that public comment is impliedly invited by reason of their conspicuous and semi-public nature. It may be said that at no time have private industries become of such startling interest to the community at large as at present in the United States." How far present-day tendencies have borne out Mr. Child's expectation of a growing sand accepted public interest in important industrial enterprises, the reader can judge for himself.

With regard to the second tendency—the increased readiness of the public to expect information about and to be heard on matters of political and social interest—Ray Stannard Baker's description of the American journalist at the Peace Conference of Versailles gives an excellent picture. Mr. Baker tells what a shock American newspaper men gave Old World diplomats because at the Paris conference they "had come, not begging, but demanding." They sat at every doorway," says Mr. Baker. "They looked over every shoulder. They wanted every resolution and report and wanted it immediately. I shall never forget the delegation of American newspaper men, led by John Nevlin, I saw come striding through that Holy of Holies, the French Foreign Office, demanding that they be admitted to the first general session of the Peace Conference. They horrified the upholders of the old methods, they desperately offended the ancient conventions, they were as rough and direct as democracy itself."

And I shall never forget the same feeling brought home to me, when Herbert Bayard Swope of the *New York World*, in the press room at the Crillon Hotel in Paris, led the discussion of the newspaper representatives who forced the conference to regard public opinion and admit newspaper men, and give out communiqués daily.

That the pressure of the public for admittance to the mysteries of foreign affairs is being felt by the nations of the world may be seen from the following dispatch published in the *New York Herald* under the date line of the *New York Herald* Bureau, Paris, January 17, 1922: "The success of Lord Riddell in getting publicity for British opinion during the Washington conference, while the French viewpoint was not stressed, may result in the appointment by the Poincaré Government of a real propaganda agent to meet the foreign newspaper men. The *Éclair* today calls on the new premier to 'find his own Lord Riddell in the French diplomatic and parliamentary world, who can give the world the French interpretation.'" Walter Lippmann of the *New York World* in his volume *Public Opinion* declares that the "significant revolution of modern times is not industrial or economic or political, but the revolution which is taking place in the art of creating consent among the governed." He goes on: "Within the life of the new generation now in control of affairs, persuasion has become a self-conscious art and a regular organ of popular government. None of us begins to understands the consequences, but it is no daring prophecy to say that the knowledge of how to create consent will alter every political premise. Under the impact of propaganda, not necessarily in the sinister meaning of the world alone, the only constants of our thinking have become variables. It is no longer possible, for example, to believe in the cardinal dogma of democracy, that the knowledge needed for the management of human affairs comes up spontaneously from the human heart. Where we act on that theory we expose ourselves to self-deception and to forms of persuasion that we cannot verify. It has been demonstrated that we cannot rely upon intuition, conscience, or the accidents of casual opinion if we are to deal with the world beyond our reach."[1]

In domestic affairs the importance of opinion not only in political decisions but in the daily industrial life of the nation may be seen from numerous incidents. In the *New York Times* of Friday, May 20, 1922, I find almost a column article with the heading "Hoover Prescribes Publicity for Coal." Among the improvements in the coal industry generally, which Mr. Hoover, according to the dispatch, anticipates from widespread, accurate and informative publicity about the industry itself, are the stimulation of industrial consumers to more regular demands, the ability to forecast more reliably the volume of demand, the ability of the consumer to "form some judgment as to the prices he should pay for coal," and the tendency to hold down over-expansion in the industry by publication of the ratio of production to capacity. Mr. Hoover concludes that really informative publicity "would protect the great majority of operators from the criticism that can only be properly leveled at the minority." Not so many years ago neither the majority nor the minority in the coal industry would have concerned itself about public criticism of the industry.

From coal to jewelry seems rather a long step, and yet in *The Jeweler's Circular*, a trade magazine, I find much comment upon the National Jewelers' Publicity Association. This association began with the simple commercial ambition of acquainting the public with "the value of jewelry merchandise for gift purposes."; now it finds itself engaged in eliminating from the public mind in general, and from the minds of legislators in particular, the impression that "the jewelry business is absolutely useless and that any money spent in a jewelry store is thrown away."

---

1. Walter Lippman, *Public Opinion*, page 248.

Not so long ago it would scarcely have occurred to any one in the jewelry industry that there was any importance to be attached to the opinion of the public on the essential or no-essential character of the jewelry industry. Today, on the other hand, jewelers find it a profitable investment to bring before the people the fact that table silver is an essential in modern life, and that without watches "the business and industries of the nation would be a sad chaos." With all the other competing interests in the world today, the question as to whether the public considers the business of manufacturing and selling jewelry essential or non-essential is a matter of the first importance to the industry.

The best examples, of course, of the increasing importance of public opinion to industries which until recently scarcely concerned themselves with the existence or non-existence of a public opinion about them, are those industries which are charged with a public interest.

In a long article about the attitude of the public towards the railroads, the *Railway Age* reaches the conclusion that the most important problem which American railroads must solve is "the problem of selling themselves to the public." Some public utilities maintain public relations departments, whose function it is to interpret the organizations to the public, as much as to interpret the public to them. The significant thing, however, is not the accepted importance of public opinion in this or the other individual industry, but the fact that public opinion is becoming cumulatively more and more articulate and therefore more important to industrial life as a whole.

The New York Central Railroad, for example, maintains a Public Relations Department under Pitt Hand, whose function it is to make it clear to the public that the railroad is functioning efficiently to serve the public in every possible way. This department studies the public and tries to discover where the railroad's service can be mended or improved, or when wrong or harmful impressions upon the public mind may be corrected.

This Public Relations Department finds it profitable not only to bring to the attention of the public the salient facts about its trains, its time tables, and its actual traveling facilities, but also to build up a broadly cooperative spirit that is indirectly of great value to itself and benefit to the public. It cooperates, for example, with such movements as the Welcome Stranger Committee of New York City in distributing literature to travelers to assist them when they reach the city. It cooperates with conventions, to the extent of arranging special travel facilities. Such aids as it affords to the directors of children's camps at the Grand Central Station are especially conspicuous for their dramatic effect on the general public.

Even a service which is in a large measure non-competitive must continually "sell" itself to the public, as evidenced by the strenuous efforts of the New York subways and elevated lines to keep themselves constantly before the people in the most favorable possible aspect. The subways strive in this regard to create a feeling of submissiveness toward inconveniences which are more or less unavoidable, and they strive likewise to fulfill such constructive programs as that of extending traffic on less frequented lines.

Let us analyze, for example, the activities of the health departments of such large cities as New York. Of recent years, Health Commissioner Royal S. Copeland and his statements have formed a fairly regular part of the day's news. Publicity is, in fact, one of the major functions of the Health Department, inasmuch as its constructive work depends to a considerable extent upon the public education it provides in combating evils and in building up a spirit of individual and group cooperation in all health matters. When the Health Department recognizes that such diseases as cancer, tuberculosis and those following malnutrition are due generally to ignorance or neglect and that amelioration or prevention will be the result of knowledge, it is the next logical step for this department to devote strenuous efforts to its public relations campaign. The department accordingly does exactly this.

Even governments today act upon the principle that it is not sufficient to govern their own citizens well and to assure the people that they are acting whole-heartedly in their behalf. They understand that the public opinion of the entire world is important to their welfare. Thus Lithuania, already noted, while it had the unbounded love and support of its own people, was nevertheless in danger of extinction because it was unknown outside of the immediate boundaries of those nations which had a personal interest in it. Lithuania was wanted by Poland; it was wanted by Russia. It was ignored by other nations. Therefore, through the aid of a public relations expert, Lithuania issued pamphlets, it paraded, it figured in pictures and motion pictures and developed a favorable sentiment throughout the world that in the end gave Lithuania its freedom.

In industry and business, of course, there is another consideration of first-rate importance, besides the danger of interference by the public in the conduct of the industry—the increasing intensity of competition. Business and sales are no longer to be had, if ever they were to be had for the asking. It must be clear to any one who has looked through the mass of advertising in street cars, subways, newspapers and magazines, and the other avenues of approach to the public, that products and services press hard upon one another in the effort to focus public attention on their offerings and to induce favorable action.

The keen competition in the selling of products for public favor makes it imperative that the seller consider other things than merely his product in trying to build up a favorable public reaction. He must either himself appraise the public mind and his relation to it or he must engage the services of an expert who can aid him to do this. He may today consider, for instance, in his sales campaign, not only the quality of his soap but the working conditions, the hours of labor, even the living conditions of the men who make it.

The public relations counsel must advise him on these factors as well as on the presentation to the public most interested in them.

In this state of affairs it is not at all surprising that industrial leaders should give the closest attention to public relations in both the broadest and the most practical concept of the term.

Large industrial groups, in their associations, have assigned a definite place to public relations bureaus.

The Trade Association Executives in New York, an association of individual executives of state, territorial or national trade associations, such as the Allied Wall Paper Industry, the American Hardware Manufacturers' Association, the American Protective Tariff League, the Atlantic Coast Shipbuilders' Association, the National Association of Credit Men, the Silk Association of America and some seventy-four others, includes among its associations' functions such activities as the following: cooperative advertising; adjustments and collections; cost accounting; a credit bureau; distribution and new markets; educational, standardization and research work; exhibits; a foreign trade bureau; house organs; general publicity; an industrial bureau; legislative work; legal aid; market reports; statistics; a traffic department; Washington representation; arbitration. It is noteworthy that forty of these associations have incorporated public relations with general publicity as a definite part of their program in furthering the interest of their organizations.

The American Telephone and Telegraph Company devotes effort to studying its pubic relations problems, not only to increase its volume of business, but also to create a cooperative spirit between itself and the public. The work of the telephone company's operators, statistics, calls, lineage, installations are given to the public in various forms. During the war and for a period afterwards its main problem was that of satisfying the public that its service was necessarily below standard because of the peculiar national conditions. The public, in response to the efforts of the company, which were analogous to a gracious personal apology, accepted more or less irksome conditions as a matter of course. Had the company not cared about the public, the public would undoubtedly have been unpleasantly insistent upon a maintenance of the pre-war standards of service.

Americans were once wont to jest about the dependence of France and Switzerland upon the tourist trade. Today we see American cities competing, as part of their public relations programs, for conventions, fairs and conferences. *The New York Times* printed some time ago an address by the governor of Nebraska, in which he told a group of advertising men that publicity had made Nebraska prosper.

The New York Herald carried an editorial recently, entitled, "It pays a state to advertise," centering about the campaign of the state of Vermont to present itself favorably to public attention. According to the editorial, the state publishes a magazine, *The Vermonter*, an attractive publication filled with interesting illustrations and well-written text. It is devoted exclusively to revealing in detail the industrial and agricultural resources of the state and to presenting Vermont's strikingly beautiful scenic attractions for the summer visitor. Similar instances of elaborate efforts, taking the form of action or the printed word, either to obtain public attention or to obtain a favorable attitude from the public for individual industries and groups of industries, will come readily to the reader's mind.

Without attempting to take too seriously an amusing story printed in a recent issue of a New York newspaper, leaders in movements and industries of modern life will be inclined to agree with the protagonist of publicity spoken of. According to the story, a man set out to prove to another that it was not so much what a man did as the way it was heralded which insures his place in history. He cited Barbara Frietchie, Evangeline, John Smith and a half dozen others as instances to prove that they are remembered not for what they did, but because they had excellent counsel on their public relations.

" 'Very good,' agreed the friend. "But show me a case where a person who has really done a big thing has been overlooked.'

" 'You know Paul Revere, of course,' he said. 'But tell me the names of the two other fellows who road that night to rouse the countryside with the news that the British were coming.'

" 'Never heard of them,' was the answer.

" 'There were three waiting to see the signal hung in the tower of the Old North Church,' he said. 'Every one of them was mounted and spurred just as Mr. Longfellow described Paul Revere. They all got the signal. They all rode and waked the farmers, spreading the warning. Afterward one of them was an officer in Washington's army, another became governor of one of the States. Not one in twenty thousand Americans ever heard the names of the other two, and there is hardly a person in America who does not know all about Revere.'

"Did Revere make history or did Longfellow?' "

CHAPTER III

THE FUNCTION OF A SPECIAL PLEADER

Public opinion has entered life at many points as a decisive factor. Men and movements whose interests will be affected by the attitude of the public are taking pains to have themselves represented in the court of public opinion by the most skillful counselors they can obtain. The business of the public relations counted is somewhat like the business of the attorney—to advise his client and to litigate his causes for him.

While the special pleader in law, the lawyer for the defense, has always been accorded a formal hearing by judge and jury, this has not been the case before the court of public opinion. Here mob psychology, the intolerance of human society for a dissenting point of view, have made it difficult and often dangerous for a man to plead for a new or unpopular cause.

The Fourth Estate, a newspaper for the makers of newspapers says: " 'Counsel on public relations' and 'director of public relations' are two terms that are being encountered more often every day. There is a familiar tinge to them, in a way, but in justice to the men who bear these titles and to the concerns which employ them, it should be said that they are—or can be—dissociated from the old idea of 'publicity man.' The very fact that many of the largest corporations in the country are recognizing the need of maintaining right relationships with the public is alone important enough to assure a fair and even favorable hearing for their public relations department.

"Whether a man is really entitled to the appellation 'counsel on public relations' or whether he should merely be called 'publicity man' rests entirely with the individual and the firm that employs him. As we see it, a man who is really counsel or director of public relations has one of the most important jobs on the roster of any concern; but a man who merely represents the old idea of getting something for nothing from publishers is about *passé*....

"So there is made plain the difference between two terms, the old and the new, both of which have occasioned much natural curiosity among newspaper men. When Napoleon said, 'Circumstance? I make circumstance,' he expressed very nearly the spirit of the public relations counsel's work. So long as this new professional branch live up to the possibilities that their title suggests, they are bound to accomplish general constructive good. Maybe they, at last, will make us forget that ingratiating though insidious individual, the publicity man."

As indicative perhaps of the growing importance of the profession, an article by Mary Swain Routzahn, in charge of the Department of Surveys and Exhibits of the Russell Sage Foundation, on "Woman's Chance as Publicity Specialist" published in the *New York Globe* of August 2, 1921, discusses the profession as one of recent development, but of such importance as to deserve the serious consideration of women who are interested in making a professional career for themselves.

The public relations counsel is first of all a student. His

field of study is the public mind. His text books for this study are the facts of life; the articles printed in newspapers and magazines, the advertisements that are inserted in publications, the billboards that line the streets, the railroads and the highways, the speeches that are delivered in legislative chambers, the sermons issuing from pulpits, anecdotes related in smoking rooms, the gossip of Wall Street, the patter of the theater and the conversation of other men who, like them, are interpreters and must listen for the clear or obscure enunciations of the public.

He brings the talent of his intuitive understanding to the aid of his practical and psychological tests and surveys. But he is not only a student. He is a practitioner with a wide range of instruments and a definite technique for their use.

First of all, there are the circumstances and events he helps to create. After that there are the instruments by which he broadcasts facts and ideas to the public; advertising, motion pictures, circular letters, booklets, handbills, speeches, meetings, parades, news articles, magazine articles and whatever other mediums there are through which public attention is reached and influenced.

Now sensitiveness to the state of mind of the public is a difficult thing to achieve or maintain. Any man can tell you with more or less accuracy and clearness his own reactions on any particular issue. But few men have the time or the interest or the training to develop a sense of what other persons think or feel abut the same issue. In his own profession the skilled practitioner is sensitive and understanding. The lawyer can tell what argument will appeal to court or jury. The salesman can tell what points to stress to his prospective buyers. The politician can tell what to emphasize to his audience, but the ability to estimate group reactions on a large scale over a wide geographic and psychological area is a specialized ability which must be developed with the same painstaking self-criticism and with the same dependence on experience that are required for the development of the clinical sense in the doctor or the surgeon.

Of course, the public relations counsel employs all those practical means of gauging the public mind which modern advertising has developed and uses. He employs the research campaign, the symposium, the survey of a particular group or of a particular state of mind as a further aid, and confirmation or modification of his own appraisals and judgments.

Charles J. Rosebault, the author of an article in the *New York Times* recently, headed "Men Who Wield the Spotlight," remarks that the competent public relations counsel has generally had some newspaper training and that the value of this training "is a keen sense of the likes and dislikes of what we call the public—that is, the average of men and women. The needle of the compass is no more sensitive to direction, nor the mercury of the thermometer to variations of heat and cold than is this expert to the influence of publicity upon the mind and emotions of the man in the street."

It is not surprising that the growing interest of the public in men and movements should have led to the spontaneous creation of the new profession.

We have presented here, in very broad outline, a picture of the fundamental work of the public relations counsel and of the fundamental conditions which have produced him. On the one hand, a complex environment of which only small, disconnected portions are available to different persons; on the other hand, the great and increasing importance either of making one's case accessible to the public mind or of determining whether that case will impinge favorably or unfavorably upon the public mind—these two conditions, taken together, have resulted inevitably in the public relations counsel. Mr. Lippmann finds in these facts the underlying reason for the existence of what he calls the "press agent." "The enormous discretion," he says, "as to what facts and what impressions shall be reported is steadily convincing every organized group of people that, whether it wishes to secure publicity or to avoid it, the exercise of discretion cannot be left to the reporter. It is safer to hire a press agent who stands between the group and the newspapers."[1]

It is clear that the popular impression of the scope and functions of the counsel on public relations must be radically revised if any accurate picture of the profession is to be looked for. The public relations counsel is the lineal descendent, to be sure, of the circus advance-man and of the semi-journalist promoter of small-part actresses. The economic conditions which have produced him, however, made his profession the important one it is today, have in themselves materially changed the character of his work.

His primary function now is not to bring his clients by chance to the public's attention, nor to extricate them form difficulties into which they have already drifted, but to advise his clients how positive results can be accomplished in the field of public relations and to keep them from drifting inadvertently into unfortunate or harmful situations. The public relations counsel will find that the conditions under which his client operates, be it a government, a manufacturer of food products or a railroad system, are constantly changing and that he

---

1. *Public Opinion* (page 342). Mr. Lippman goes on to say that "having hired him, the temptation to exploit his strategic position is very great." As to that aspect of the situation, see later chapters.

must advise modifications in policy in accordance with such changes in the public point of view. As such, the public relations counsel must be alive to the events of the day—not only the events that are printed but the events which are forming hour by hour, as reported in the words that are spoken on the street, in the smoking cars, in the school room, or expressed in any of the other forms of thought communication that make up public opinion.

So long as the press remains the greatest single medium for reaching the public mind, the work of the public relations counsel will necessarily have close contacts with the work of the journalist. He transmits his ideas, however, through all those mediums which help to build public opinion—the radio, the lecture platform, advertising, the stage, the motion picture, the mails. On the other hand, he is becoming today as much of an adviser on actions as he is the communicator of these actions to the public.

The public relations consultant is ideally a constructive force in the community. The results of his work are often accelerated interest in matters of value and importance to the social, economic or political life of the community.

The public relations counsel is the pleader to the public point of view. He acts in this capacity as a consultant both in interpreting the public to his client and in helping to interpret his client to the public. He helps to mould the action of his client as well as to mould public opinion.

His profession is in a state of evolution. His future must depend as much upon the growing realization by the public of the responsibility to the public of individuals, institutions and organizations as upon the public relations counsel's own realization of the importance of his work.

PART II

THE GROUP AND HERD

CHAPTER I

WHAT CONSTITUTES PUBLIC OPINION?

The character and origins of public opinion, the factors that make up the individual mind and the group mind must be understood if the profession of public relations counsel is to be intelligently practiced and its functions and possibilities accurately estimated. Society must understand the fundamental character of the work he is doing, if for no other reason than its own welfare.

The public relations counsel works with that vague, little-understood, indefinite material called public opinion.

Public opinion is a term describing an ill-defined, mercurial and changeable group of individual judgments. Public opinion is the aggregate result of individual opinions —now uniform, now conflicting—of the men and women who make up society or any group of society. In order to understand public opinion, one must go back to the individual who makes up the group.

The mental equipment of the average individual consists of a mass of judgments on most of the subjects which touch his daily physical or mental life. These judgments are the tools of his daily being and yet they are his judgments, not on a basis of research and logical deduction, but for the most part dogmatic expressions accepted on the authority of his parents, his teachers, his church, and of his social, his economic and other leaders.

The public relations counsel must understand the social implications of an individual's thoughts and actions. Is it, for example, purely an accident that a man belongs to one church rather than another or to any other church at all? Is it an accident that makes Boston women prefer brown eggs and New York women white eggs? What are the factors that work in favor of conversion of a man from one political party to another or form one type of food to another?

Why do certain communities resist the prohibition law— why do others abide by it? Why is it difficult to start a new party movement—or to fight cancer? Why is it difficult to fight for sex education? Why does the free trader denounce protectionism, and vice versa?

If we had to form our own judgments on every matter, we should all have to find out many things for ourselves which we now take for granted. We should not cook our food or live in houses—in fact, we should revert to primitive living.

The public relations counsel must deal with the fact that persons who have little knowledge of a subject almost invariably form definite and positive judgments upon that subject.

"If we examine the mental furniture of the average man," says William Trotter, the author of a comprehensive study of the social psychology of the individual,[1] "we shall find it made up of a vast number of judgments of a very precise kind upon subjects of very great variety, complexity, and difficulty. He will have fairly settled views upon the origin and nature of the universe, and upon what he will

1. William Trotter, *Instincts of the Herd in Peace and War*, (page 36).

probably call its meaning; he will have conclusions as to what is to happen to him at death and after, as to what is and what should be the basis of conduct. He will know how the country should be governed, and why it is going to the dogs, why this piece of legislation is good and that bad. He will have strong views upon military and naval strategy, the principles of taxation, the use of alcohol and vaccination, the treatment of influenza, the prevention of hydrophobia, upon municipal trading, the teaching of Greek, upon what is permissible in art, satisfactory in literature, and hopeful in science.

"The bulk of such opinions must necessarily be without rational basis, since many of them are concerned with problems admitted by the expert to be still unsolved, while as to the rest it is clear that the training and experience of no average man can qualify him to have any opinion upon them at all. The rational method adequately used would have told him that on the great majority of these questions there could be for him but one attitude—that of suspended judgment."

The reader will recall from his own experience an almost infinite number of instances in which the amateur has been fully prepared to deliver expert advice and to give final judgment in matters upon which his ignorance is patent to every one except himself.

In the Middle Ages, society was convinced that there were witches. People were so positive that they burned people whom they suspected of witchcraft. Today there is an equal number of people who believe just as firmly, one way or the other, about spiritualism and spirits. They do not burn mediums. But people who have made no research of the subject pass strong denunciatory judgments. Others, no better informed, consider mediums divinely inspired. Not so long ago every intelligent man knew that the world was flat. Today the average man has a belief just as firm and unknowing in the mysterious force which he has heard called atomic energy.

It is axiomatic that men who know little are often intolerant of a point of view that is contrary to their own. The bitterness that has been brought about by arguments on public questions is proverbial. Lovers have been parted by bitter quarrels on theories of pacificism or militarism; and when an argument upon an abstract question engages opponents they often desert the main line of arguments in order to abuse each other.

How often this is true can be seen from the congressional records of controversies in which the personal attack supersedes logic. In a recent fight against the proposed tariff measures, a protagonist of protection published long vindictive statements, in which he tried to confound the character and the disinterestedness of his opponents. Logically his discussion should have been based only upon the sound economic, social and political value of the bill as presented.

A hundred leading American bankers, businessmen, professional men and economists united in public disapproval of this plan. They stated their opinion that the "American" Valuation Plan, as it was called, would endanger the prosperity of the country, that it would be inimical to our foreign relations and that it would injure the welfare of every country with whom our commercial and industrial ties were at all close. This group was a broadly representative group of men and women, yet the chairman of the Ways and Means Committee accused all these people of acting upon motives of personal gain and lack of patriotism. Prejudice superseded logic.

Intolerance is almost inevitably accompanied by a natural and true inability to comprehend or make allowance for opposite points of view. The skilled scientist who may be receptive to any promising suggestion in his own field may outside of his own field be found quite unwilling to make any attempt at understanding a point of view contrary to his own. In politics, for example, his understanding of the problem may be fragmentary, yet he will enter excitedly into discussions on bonus and ship subsidy, of which he has made no study. We find here with significant uniformity what one psychologist has called "logic-proof compartments."

The logic-proof compartment has always been with us. Scientists have lost their lives through refusing to see flaws in their theories. Intelligent mothers give food to their babies that they would manifestly forbid other mothers to give their children. Especially significant is the tendency of races to maintain religious beliefs and customs long after these have lost their meaning. Dietary laws, hygienic laws, even laws based upon geographical conditions that have been changed for more than a thousand years are still maintained in the logic-proof compartment of dogmatic adherence. There is a story that certain missionaries give money to heathen at the time of conversion and that the heathen, having got their money, bathe away their conversion in sacred streams.

The characteristic of the human mind to adhere to its beliefs is excellently summarized in the volume by Mr. Trotter to which reference has been made before. "It is clear,"[2] says Mr. Trotter, "at the outset that these beliefs are invariably regarded as rational and defended as such, while, the position of one who holds contrary views is held to be obviously unreasonable.

"The religious man accuses the atheist of being shallow and irrational, and is met by a similar reply. To the Conser-

---

2. William Trotter, *Instincts of the Herd in Peace and War*, (page 36-37).

vative the amazing thing about the Liberal is his incapacity to see reason and accept the only possible solution of public problems. Examination reveals the fact that the differences are not due to the commission of the mere mechanical fallacies of logic, since these are easily avoided, even by the politician, and since there is no reason to believe that one party in such controversies is less logical than the other. The difference is due rather to the fundamental assumptions of the antagonists being hostile, and these assumptions are derived from herd-suggestions; to the Liberal certain basal conceptions have acquired the quality of instinctive truth, have become *a priori* syntheses, because of the accumulated suggestions to which he has been exposed; and a similar explanation applies to the atheist, the Christian, and the Conservative. Each, it is important to remember, finds in consequence the rationality of his position flawless and is quite incapable of detecting in it the fallacies which are obvious to his opponent, to whom that particular series of assumptions has not been rendered acceptable by herd suggestion."

Thus the public relations counsel has to consider the *a prori* judgment of any public he deals with before counseling any step that would modify those things in which the public has established belief.

It is seldom effective to call names or to attempt to discredit the beliefs themselves. The counsel on public relations, after examination of the sources of established beliefs, must either discredit the old authorities or create new authorities by making articulate a mass opinion against the old belief or in favor of the new.

CHAPTER II

IS PUBLIC OPINION STUBBORN OR
MALLEABLE?

There is a divergence of opinion as to whether the public mind is malleable or stubborn—whether it is a passive or an active element. On the one hand is the profound belief that "you can't change human nature." On the other hand is the equally firm assurance that certain well-defined institutions modify and alter public opinion.

There is a uniformity of opinion in this country upon many issues. When this uniformity accords with our own beliefs we call it an expression of the public conscience. When, however, it runs contrary to our beliefs we call it regimentation of the public mind and are inclined to ascribe it to insidious propaganda.

Uniformity is, in fact, largely natural and only partly artificial. Public opinion may be as much the producer of "insidious propaganda" as its product. Naturally enough, where broad ideas are involved, criticisms of the state of the public's mind and of its origin come most frequently from groups that are out of sympathy with the accepted point of view. They find the public unreceptive to their point of view, and justly or unjustly they attribute this to the influence of antagonistic interests upon the public mind.

These groups see the press, the lecture platform, the schools, the advertisements, the churches, the radio, the motion picture screen, the magazines daily reaching millions. They see that the preponderant point of view in most, if not all, these institutions conforms to the preponderant state of mind of the public.

They argue from the one to the other and reach their conclusions without much difficulty. They do not stop to think that agreement in point of view between the public and these institutions may often be the result of the control exercised by the public mind over these institutions.

Many outside forces, however, do go to influence pubic opinion. The most obvious of these forces are parental influence, the school room, the press, motion pictures, advertising, magazines, lectures, the church, the radio.

To answer the question as to the stubbornness or malleability of the public, let us analyze the press in its relation to public opinion, since the press stands preeminent among the various institutions which are commonly designated as leaders or molders of the public mind. By the press, in this instance, I mean the daily press. Americans are a newspaper-reading public. They have become accustomed to look to their morning and evening papers for the news of the world and for the opinions of their leaders. And while the individual newspaper reader does not give a very considerable portion of his day to this occupation, many persons find time to read more than one newspaper every day.

It is not surprising that the man who is outside the current of prevailing public opinion should regard the daily press as a coercive force.

Discussions of the public's reaction to the press are two-sided, just as are the discussions of the influence of the pulpit or other forces. Some authorities hold that the public mind is stubborn in regard to the press and that the press has little influence upon it. There are graphic instances of the stubbornness of the public point of view. A most interesting example is the reelection of Mayor Haylan of New York by an overwhelming majority in the face of the opposition of all but two of the metropolitan dailies. It is also noteworthy that in 1909, Gaynor was elected Mayor New York with every paper except one opposing his candidacy. Likewise, Mayor Mitchel of New York was defeated for reelection in 1917, although all the New York papers except two Hearst papers and the *New York Call* supported him. In Boston, in a recent election, a man was elected as mayor who had been convicted of a penal offense, and elected in the face of the practically united opposition of all the newspapers of that city. How would such authors as Everett Dean Martin, Walter Lippmann and Upton Sinclair explain these incidents? How, on the theory of the regimentation of the public mind by the daily press, can such thinkers explain the sharpness with which the public sometimes rejects the advocacies of a united press? These instances are not frequent; but they show that other influences beside the press enter into the making of a public opinion and that these forces must never be disregarded in the estimate of the quality and stability of a prevalent public opinion.

Francis E. Leupp, writing in the *Atlantic Monthly* for February, 1910, on "The Waning Power of the Press," remarks that Mayor Gaynor's comments shortly after his election in 1909 "led up to the conclusion that in our common sense generation nobody cares what the newspapers say." Mr. Leupp continues: "Unflattering as such a verdict may be, probably the majority of a community if polled as a jury would concur in it. The airy dismissal of some proposition as 'mere newspaper talk' is heard at every social gathering until one who is brought up to regard the press as a mighty factor in modern civilization is tempted to wonder whether it has actually lost the power it used to wield among us."

And H.L. Mencken, writing in the same magazine for March, 1914, declares that "one of the principal marks of an educated man, indeed, is the fact that he does *not* take his opinions from newspapers—not, at any rate, from the militant, crusading newspapers. On the contrary, his attitude toward them is almost always one of frank cynicism, with indifference as its mildest form and contempt as its commonest. He knows that they are constantly falling into false reasoning about the things within his personal knowledge,—that is, within the narrow circle of his special education,—and so he assumes that they make the same, or even worse, errors about other things, whether intellectual or moral. This assumption, it may be said, is quite justified by the facts."

The second point of view holds that the daily press and the other leading forces merely accept, reflect and intensify established public opinion and are, therefore, responsible for the uniformity of public reaction. A vivid statement of the point of view of the man who typifies this group is found in Everett Dean Martin's volume on *The Behavior of Crowds*. He says:[1] "The modern man has in the printing press a wonderfully effective means for perpetuating crowd-movements and keeping great masses of people constantly under the sway of certain crowd-ideas. Every crowd-group has its magazines, press agents, and special 'literature' with which it continually

---

1. Page 45.

harangues its members and possible converts. Many books, and especially certain works of fiction of the 'best seller' type, are clearly reading mob phenomena."

There is a third group which perhaps comes nearer the truth, which holds that the press, just as other mediums of education or dissemination, brings about a very definite change in public opinion. A most graphic illustration of what such mediums can do to change opinions upon fundamental and important matters is the woman suffrage question and its victory over established points of view. The press, the pulpit, the lecture platform, the motion pictures and the other mediums for reaching the public brought about a complete popular conversion. Other examples of the change that may be brought about in public opinion in this way, by such institutions of authority, is the present attitude towards birth control and towards health education.

Naturally the press, like other institutions which present facts or opinions, is restricted, often unconsciously, sometimes consciously, by various controlling conditions. Certain people talk of the censorship enacted by the prejudices and predispositions of the public itself. Some, such as Upton Sinclair, ascribe to the advertisers a conscious and powerful control of publications. Others, like Walter Lippmann, find that an effective barrier between the public and the event exists in the powerful influence which, he says, is exerted in certain cases on the press by the so-called quality public which the newspapers' advertisers which to reach and among whom the newspapers must circulate if the advertising is to be successful. Mr. Lippmann observes that although such a restriction may exist, much of what may be attributed to censorship in the newspaper, often is actually inadequate presentation of the events it seeks to describe.

On this point he says:[2] "It follows that in the reporting of strikes, the easiest way is to let the news be uncovered by the overt act, and to describe the event as the story of the interference with the reader's life. This is where his attention is first aroused and his interest most easily enlisted. A great deal, I think myself, of the crucial part of what looks to the worker and the reformer as deliberate misrepresentation on the part of newspapers, is the direct outcome of a practical difficulty in uncovering the news, and the emotional difficulty of making distinct facts interesting unless, as Emerson says, we can 'perceive' (them) and can 'set about translating (them) at once into parallel facts.' "

In view then of the possibility of a malleable public opinion the counsel on public relations, desiring to obtain a hearing for any given cause, simply utilizes existent channels to obtain expression for the point of view he represents. How this is done will be considered later.

Because of the importance of channels of thought communication, it is vital for the public relations counsel to study carefully the relationship between public opinion and the organs that maintain it or that influence it to change. We shall look into this interaction and its effect in the next chapter.

---

2. *Public Opinion* (page 350).

CHAPTER III

THE INTERACTION OF PUBLIC OPINION
WITH THE FORCES THAT HELP TO MAKE IT

The public and the press, or for that matter, the public and any force that modifies pubic opinion, interact. Action and interaction are continually going on between the forces projected out to the public and the public itself. The public relations counsel must understand this fact in its broadest and most detailed implications. He must understand not only what these various forces are, but he must be able to evaluate their relative powers with fair accuracy. Let us consider again the case of a newspaper, as representative of other mediums of communications.

"We print," says the *New York Times*, "all news that's fit to print." Immediately the question arises (as Elmer Davis, the historian of the *Times* tells us that it did when the motto was first adopted) what news *is* fit to print? By what standard is the editorial decision reached which includes one kind of news and excludes another kind? The *Times* itself has not been, in its long and conspicuously successful career, entirely free from difficulties on this point.

Thus in "The History of the *New York Times*," Mr. Davis feels the need for justifying the extent to which that paper featured Theodore Tilton's action against the Rev. Henry Ward Beecher for alienation of Mrs. Tilton's affections and his conduct with her. Mr. Davis says (pages 124-125): "No doubt a good many readers of the *Times* thought the paper was giving an undue amount of space to this chronicle of sin and suffering. Those complaints come often enough even in these days from readers who appreciate the paper's general reluctance to display news of this sort, and wonder why a good general rule should occasionally be violated. But there was a reason in the Beecher case, as there has usually been a reason in similar affairs since. Dr. Beecher was one of the most prominent clergymen in the country; there was a natural curiosity as to whether he was practicing what he preached. One of the counsel at the trial declared that 'all Christendon was hanging on its outcome.' Full reporting off its course was not a mere pandering to vulgar curiosity, but a recognition of the value of the case as news."

The simple fact that such a slogan can exist and be accepted is for our purpose an important point. Somewhere there must be a standard to which the editors of the *Times* can conform, as well as a larger clientele of constant readers to whom that standard is satisfactory. "Fit" must be defined by the editors of the *Times* in a way which meets with the approval of enough persons to enable the paper to maintain its reading public. As soon, however, as the definition is attempted, difficulties arise.

Professor W.G. Bleyer, in an article in his book on journalism, first stresses the importance of completeness in the news columns of a paper, then goes on to say that "the only important limitations to completeness are those imposed by the commonly accepted ideas of decency embodied in the words, 'All the news that's fit to print' and by the rights of privacy. Carefully edited newspapers discriminate between what the public is entitled to know and what an individual has a right to keep private."

On the other hand, when Professor Bleyer attempts to define what news is fit to print and what the public is entitled to know, he discusses generalizations capable of wide and frequently inconsistent interpretation. "News," says he, "is anything timely which is significant to newspaper readers in their relations to the community, the state and the nation."

Who is to determine what is significant and what is not? Who is to decide which of the individual's relations to the community are safeguarded by his right of privacy and which are not? Such a definition tells us nothing more definite than does the slogan which it attempts to define. We must look further for a standard by which these definitions are applied. There must be a consensus of public opinion on which the newspaper falls back for its standards.

The truth is that while it appears to be forming the public opinion on fundamental matters, the press is often conforming to it.

It is the office of the public relations counsel to determine the interaction between the public, and the press and the other mediums affecting public opinion. It is as important to conform to the standards of the organ which projects ideas as it is to present to this organ such ideas as will conform to the fundamental understanding and appreciation of the public to which they are ultimately to appeal. There is as much truth in the proposition that the public leads institutions as in the contrary proposition that the institutions lead the public.

As an illustration of the manner in which newspapers are inclined to accept the judgments of their readers in presenting material to them, we have this anecdote which Rollo Ogden tells in the *Atlantic Monthly* for July, 1906, about a letter which Wendell Phillips wished to have published in a Boston paper.

"The editor read it over, and said, 'Mr. Phillips, that is a very good and interesting letter, and I shall be glad to publish it; but I wish you would consent to strike out the last paragraph.'

"'Why,' said Phillips, 'that paragraph is the precise thing for which I wrote the whole letter. Without that it would be pointless.'

"'Oh, I see that,' replied the editor; 'and what you say is perfectly true! I fully agree with it all myself. Yet it is one of those things which will not do to say publicly. However, if you insist upon it, I will publish it as it stands.'

"It was published the next morning, and along with it a short editorial reference to it, saying that a letter from Mr. Phillips would be found in another column, and that it was extraordinary that so keen a mind as his should have fallen into the palpable absurdity contained in the last paragraph."

Recognition of this fact comes from a number of different sources. H. L. Mencken recognizes that the public runs the press as much as the press runs the public.

"The primary aim of all of them," says Mr. Mencken,[1] "not less when they play the secular Iokanaan than when they play the mere newsmonger, was to please the crowd, and to give a good show; and the way they set about giving that good show was by first selecting a deserving victim, and then putting him magnificently to the torture.

"This was their method when they were performing for their own profit only, when their one motive was to make the public read their paper; but it was still their motive when they were battling bravely and unselfishly for the public good, and

1. *Atlantic Monthly*, March, 1914.

so discharging the highest duty of their profession."

There are interesting, if somewhat obscure examples of the complementary working of various forces. In the field of the motion pictures, for example, the producers, the actors, and the press, in their support, have continually waged a battle against censorship. Undoubtedly censorship of the motion pictures is in its practical workings an economic and artistic handicap. Censorship, however, will continue in spite of the producers as long as there is a willingness on the part of the public to accept this censorship. The public, on the whole, has refused to join the fight against censorship, because there is a more or less articulate belief that children, if not women, should be protected from seeing shocking sights, such as murders visibly enacted, the taking of drugs, immoralities and other acts which might offend or suggest harmful imitation.

"Damaged Goods," before its presentation to America in 1913, was analyzed by the public relations counsel, who helped to produce the play. He recognized that unless that part of the public sentiment which believed in education and truth could be lifted from that part of public opinion which condemned the mentioning of sex matters, "Damaged Goods" would fail. The producers, therefore, did not try to educate the public by presenting this play as such, but allowed group leaders amd groups interested in education to come to the support of Brieux's drama and, in a sense, to sponsor the production.

Proof that the public and the institutions that make public opinion interact is shown in instances in which books were stifled because of popular disapproval at one time and then brought forward by popular demand at a later time when public opinion had altered. Religious and very early scientific works are among such books.

A more recent instance is the announcement made by

Judge, a weekly magazine, that it would support the fight for light wine and beer. *Judge* took this stand because it believed in the principle of personal freedom and also because it deemed that public sentiment was in favor of light wine and beer as a substitute for absolute prohibition. *Judge* believed its stand would please its readers.

Presumably writing of newspaper morality, Mr. Mencken, in his article just quoted, finds at the end of it that he has "written of popular morality very copiously, and of newspaper morality very little.

"But," says Mr. Mencken, "as I have said before, the one is the other. The newspaper must adapt its pleading to its clients' moral limitation just as the trial lawyer also must adapt *his* pleading to the jury's limitations. Neither may like the job, but both must face it to gain the larger end."

Writing on the other hand from the point of view of the man who feels that the public taste requires no justification, Ralph Pulitzer nevertheless agrees with Mr. Mencken that the opinion of the press is set by the public; and he justifies "muckraking"[2] by finding it neither "extraordinary nor culpable that people and press should be more interested in the polemical than in the platitudinous; in blame than in painting the lily; in attack than in sending laudatory coals to Newcastle."

Even Mr. Leupp[3] concludes that "whatever we may say of the modern press on its less commendable side, we are bound to admit that newspapers, like governments, fairly reflect the people they serve. Charles Dudley Warner once went so far as to say that no matter how objectionable the character of a

---

2. *Atlantic Monthly*, March, 1914.
3. Frances E. Leupp, "The Waning Power of the Press," *Atlantic Monthly*, July 1910.

THE GROUP AND HERD

paper may be, it is always a trifle better than the patrons on whom it relies for its support."

Similarly, from an unusually wide experience on a paper as highly considered, perhaps, as any in America, Rollo Ogden claims this give and take between the public and the press is vital to a just conception of American journalism.

"The editor does not nonchalantly project his thoughts into the void. He listens for the echo of his words. His reaction to his supporters is not unlike Gladstone's definition of the intimate connection between the orator and his audience. As the speaker gets from his hearers in mist what he gives back in shower, so the newspaper receives from the public as well as it gives back to it. Too often it gets as dust what it gives back as mud; but that does not alter the relations. Action and reaction are all the while going on between the press and its patrons.

Hence it follows that the responsibility for the more crying evils of journalism must be divided."[4]

This same interaction goes on in connection with all the other forces that mould public opinion. The preacher upholds the ideals of society. He leads his flock wither they indicate a willingness to be led. Ibsen creates a revolution when society is ripe for it. The public responds to finer music and better motion pictures and demands improvements. "Give the people what they want" is only half sound. What they want and what they get are fused by some mysterious alchemy. The press, the lecturer, the screen and the public lead and are led by each other.

---

4. Rollo Ogden, "Some Aspects of Journalism," *Atlantic Monthly*, July, 1906.

CHAPTER IV

THE POWER OF INTERACTING FORCES
THAT GO TO MAKE UP PUBLIC OPINION

The influence of any force which attempts to modify public opinion depends upon the success with which it is able to enlist established points of view. A middle ground exists between the hypothesis that the public is stubborn and the hypothesis that it is malleable. To a large degree the press, the schools, the churches, motion pictures, advertising, the lecture platform and radio all conform to the demands of the public. But to an equally large degree the public responds to the influence of these very same mediums of communication.

Some analysts believe that the public has no opinions except those which various institutions provide ready made for it. From Mr. Mencken and others it would almost seem to follow that newspapers and other mediums have no standards except those which the public provides, and that therefore they are substantially without influence upon the public mind. The truth of the matter, as I have pointed out, lies somewhere between these two extreme positions.

In other words, the public relations counsel who thinks clearly on the problem of public opinion and public relations will credit the two factors of public opinion respectively with their influence and effectiveness in mutual interaction.

Ray Stannard Baker says[1] that "while there was a gesture of unconcern, of don't care what they say, on the part of the leaders (of the Versailles conference), no aspect of the conference in reality worried them more than the news, opinions, guesses that went out by scores of thousands of words every night, and the reactions which came back so promptly from them. The problems of publicity consumed an astonishing amount of time, anxiety and discussion among the leaders of the conference. It influenced the entire procedure, it was partly instrumental in driving the four heads of States finally into small secret conferences. The full achievement of publicity on one occasion—Wilson's Italian note—nearly broke up the conference and overturned a government. The bare threat of it, upon other occasions, changed the course of the discussion. Nothing concerned the conference more than what democracy was gong to do with diplomacy."

For like causes we find great industries—motion pictures being one and organized baseball another—appointing as directors of their activities men prominent in public life, doing this to assure the public of the honest and social-minded conduct of their members. The Franklin Roosevelts are in this class, the Will Hayes and the Landises.

A striking example of this interaction is illustrated in what occurred at the Hague Conference a few years ago. The effect of the Hague Conference's conduct upon the public was such that officials were forced to open the Conference doors to the representatives of newspapers. On June 16th, 1922, a note came from The Hague by the Associated Press that Foreign Minister Van Karnebeek of Holland capitulated to the world's desire to be informed of what was going on by ad-

---

1. "Publicity at Paris," *New York Times*, April 2, 1922.

mitting correspondents. Early announcement that "the press cannot be admitted" was, according to the report, followed by anxious emissaries begging the journalists to have patience. Editorials printed in Holland pointed out that the best way to insure public cooperation was to take the public into its confidence. Minister van Karnebeek, who had been at Washington, was thoroughly awake to the invaluable service the press of the world rendered there. One editorial here pointed out that public statements "were used by the diplomats themselves as a happy means of testing popular opinion upon the various projects offered in council. How many 'trial balloons' were sent up in this fashion, nobody can recall. Nevertheless each delegation maintained clipping bureaus, which were brought up to date every morning and which gave the delegates accurate information as to the state of mind at home. Thus it came about that world opinion was ready and anxious to receive the finished work of the conference and that it was prompt to bring individual recalcitrant groups into line."

Let me quote from the *New York Evening Post* of July, 1922, as to the important interaction of these forces: "The importance of the press in guiding public opinion and the cooperation between the members of the press and the men who express public opinion in action, which has grown up since the Peace Conference at Paris, were stress by Lionel Curtis, who arrived on the *Adriatic*, yesterday to attend the Institute of Politics, which opens on July 27 at Williamstown. 'Perhaps for the first time in history,' he said, 'the men whose business it is to make public opinion were collected for some months under the same roof with the officials whose task in life is the actual conduct of foreign affairs. In the long run, foreign policy is determined by public opinion. It was impossible in Paris not to be impressed by the immense advantage of bringing into close contact the writers who, through the press, are making public opinion, and the men who have to express their opinion in actual policy.' "

Harvard University, likewise, appreciating the power of pubic opinion over its own activities, has recently appointed a counsel on public relations to make its aims clear to the public.

The institutions which make public opinion conform to the demands of the public. The public responds to an equally large degree to these institutions. Such fights as that made by *Collier's Weekly* for pure food control show this.

The Safety First movement, by its use of every form of appeal, from poster to circular, from lecture to law enforcement, from motion pictures to "safety weeks," is bringing about a gradual change in the attitude of a safety-deserving public towards the taking of unnecessary risks.

The Rockefeller Foundation, confronted with the serous problem of the hookworm in the South and in other localities, has brought about a change in the habits of large sections of rural populations by analysis, investigation, applied medical principles, and public education.

The molder of public opinion must enlist the established point of view. This is true of the press as well as of other forces. Mr. Mencken mixes cynicism and truth when he declares that the chief difficulty confronting a newspaper which tries to carry out independent and thoughtful policies "does not lie in the direction of the board of directors, but in the direction of the public which buys the paper."[2]

The New York Tribune, as an example of editorial bravery, points out in an advertisement published May 23, 1922, that though "news knows no order in the making" and though "a

---

2. H.L. Mencken, on Journalism, *The Nation*, April 26, 1922.

newspaper must carry the news, both pleasant and unpleasant," nevertheless, it is the duty of any newspaper to realize that there is a possibility of selective action, and that "in times of stress and bleak despair a newspaper has a hard and fast duty to perform in keeping up the morale of the community."

Indeed, the instances are frequent and accessible to the recollection of any reader in which newspapers have consciously maintained a point of view toward which the public is either hostile or cold.

Occasionally, of course, even the established point of view is alterable. The two Baltimore *Suns* do brave their public and have been braving their public for some time, not entirely without success. As severe a critic as Oswald Garrison Villard points out that though modern Baltimore is a difficult city to serve, yet the two Suns have courageously and consistently stood for the policies of their editors and have refused to yield to pressure from any source. To the public relations counsel this is a striking illustration of the give and take between the public and the institutions which attempt to mould public opinion. The two interact upon each other, so that it is sometimes difficult to tell which is one and which is the other.

The *World* and the *Evening World of New York*, pride themselves upon the following campaigns which are listed in *The World Almanac* of 1922. They illustrate this interaction.

> *"Conference on Limitation of Armament Grew From 'World's' Plea*
>
> "Bearing in mind in 1921 the injunction of its founder, Joseph Pulitzer, to fight always for progress and reform, and having led the campaign for disarmament in advance of any other demand therefor, the

World covered the Washington Conference on Limitation of Armament in a comprehensive way....

"Measures Advocated by 'World' Made Law

"During the 1921 session of the New York Legislature many measures advocated by the *World* were enacted. One of the paper's chief achievements was the passage of a resolution broadening the power of the Lockwood Housing Committee, enabling it to inquire into high finance as related to the building trades situation.

"The *World* was instrumental in obtaining the Anti-Theater Ticket Spectacular Law. It also brought about a change in bills to abolish the Daylight-Saving Law so that municipalities might enact their own daylight-saving ordinances. It was successful in its campaign against the search-and-seizure and other drastic features of the State Prohibition Enforcement Law.

"The 'World' Told Facts about Ku Klux Klan

"The *World* on September 6 commenced the publication of a series of articles telling the truth about the Ku Klux Klan. Twenty-six newspapers, in widely separated sections of the United States, joined the *World* in the publication; some had been invited to participate, others requested the *World* to let them use the articles. All these newspapers realized that the only motive back of the *World's* publication was public service. It was their desire to share in this service, and the *World* is proud that they asked only assurance of its traditional accuracy and fairness before they saw their way clear to cooperation.

"The *World* is proud that the completed record shows no evidence either that it was terrified by threats or was goaded by abuse into departures from its object of presenting the facts honestly and without exaggeration.

"Changes in Motor Vehicle Laws

"As a result of a crusade to lessen automobile fatalities in New York City and State, the *World* won victory when changes in the motor vehicle laws were made. The paper printed exclusive stories giving the motor and license numbers of cars stolen daily in this city, and started a campaign against outlaw taxicabs and financially irresponsible drivers and owners.

" 'Evening World's' Achievements

"The *Evening World* continued its campaign against the coal monopoly and the high coal prices charged in New York City—a state of affairs that has been constantly and vigorously exposed in *Evening World* columns. After consultation with leading Senators in Washington, several bills were introduced in Congress to alleviate the conditions."

I am letting the *World* speak for itself merely as an example of what many splendid newspapers have accomplished as leaders in public movements. The *New York Evening Post* is another example, it having long led popular demand for vocational guidance and control.

The public relations counsel cannot base his work merely upon the acceptance of the principle that the public and its authorities interact. He must go deeper than that and discover why it is that a public opinion exists independently of church, school, press, lecture platform and motion picture screen—how far this public opinion affects these institutions and how far these institutions affect public opinion. He must discover what the stimuli are to which public opinion responds most readily.

Study of the mirrors of the public mind—the press, the motion pictures, the lecture platform and the others—reveal to him what their standards are and those of the groups they reach. This is not enough, however. To his understanding of what he actually can measure he must add a thorough knowledge of the principles which govern individual and group action. A fundamental study of group and individual psychology is required before the public relations counsel can determine how readily individuals or groups will accept modifications of viewpoints or policies, which they have already imposed upon their respective mediums.

No idea or opinion is an isolated factor. It is surrounded and influenced by precedent, authority, habit and all the other human motivations.

For a lucid conception of the functions, power and social utility of the public relations counsel it is vitally important to have a clear grasp of the fundamentals with which he must work.

CHAPTER V

AN UNDERSTANDING OF THE FUNDMEN-TALS OF PUBLIC MOTIVATION IS NECESSARY TO THE WORK OF THE PUBLIC RELATIONS COUNSEL

Before defining the fundamental motivations of society, let me mention those outward signs on which psychologists base their study of conditions.

Psychological habits, or as Mr. Lippmann calls them, "stereotypes," are shorthand by which human effort is minimized. They are so clearly and commonly understood that every one will immediately respond to the mention of the stereotype within his personal experience. The words "capitalist" or "boy scout" bring out definite images to the hearer. These images are more comprehensible than detailed descriptions. Chorus girl, woman lawyer, politician, detective, financier are clean-cut concepts and capable of definition. We all have stereotypes which minimize not only our thinking habits but also the ordinary routine of life.

Mr. Lippmann finds that the stereotypes at the center of the code by which various sections of the public live, "largely determine what group of facts we shall see and in what light we shall see them." That is why, he says "with the best will in the world, the news policy of a journal tends to support its editorial policy, why a capitalist sees one set of facts and certain aspects of human nature—literally sees them; his socialist opponent another set and other aspects, and why each regards the other as unreasonable or perverse, when the real difference between them is a difference of perception. That difference is imposed by the difference between the capitalist and socialist pattern of stereotypes. 'There are no classes in America,' writes an American editor. 'The history of all hitherto existing society is the history of class struggles,' says the Communist Manifesto. If you have the editor's pattern in your mind, you will see vividly the facts that confirm it, vaguely and ineffectively those that contradict. If you have the communist pattern, you will not only look for different things, but you will see with a totally different emphasis what you and the editor happen to see in common."

The stereotype is the basis of a large part of the work of the public relations counsel. Let us try to inquire where the stereotype originates—why it is so influential and why from a practical standpoint it is so tremendously difficult to affect or change stereotypes or to attempt to substitute one set of stereotypes for another.

Mr. Martin attempts to answer questions such as these in his volume on *The Behavior of Crowds*. By "crowds" Mr. Martin does not mean merely a physical aggregation of a number of persons. To Mr. Martin the crowd is rather a state of mind, "the peculiar mental condition which sometimes occurs when people think and act together, either immediately where the members of the group are present and in close contact, or remotely, as when people think as when they affect one another in a certain way through the medium of an organization, a party or sect, the press, etc."

Motives of social behavior are based on individual instincts. Individual instincts, on the other hand, must yield to group needs. Mr. Martin pictures society as an aggregation of people who have sacrificed individual freedom in order to remain within the group. This sacrifice of freedom on the part of individuals in the group leads its members to resist all efforts at fundamental changes in the group code. Because all have made certain sacrifices, reasons are developed why such sacrifices must be insisted upon at all times. The "logic-proof" compartment is the result of this unwillingness to accept changes.

"What has been so painstakingly built up is not to be lightly destroyed. Each group, therefore, within itself, considers its own standards ultimate and indisputable, and tends to dismiss all contrary or different standards as indefensible.

"Even an honest, critical understanding of the demands of the opposing crowd is discouraged, possibly because it is rightly felt that the critical habit of mind is as destructive of one crowd-complex as the other, and the old crowd prefers to remain intact and die in the last ditch rather than risk dissolution, even with the promise of averting a revolution. Hence the Romans were willing to believe that the Christians worshipped the head of an ass. The medieval Catholics, even at Leo's court, failed to grasp the meaning of the outbreak in North Germany. Thousands saw in the reformation only the alleged fact that the monk Luther wanted to marry a wife...."[1]

The main satisfaction, Mr. Martin thinks, which the individual derives from his group association is the satisfaction of his vanity through the creation of an enlarged self-importance.

The Freudian theories upon which Mr. Martin relies very largely for his argument lead to the conclusion that what Mr. Henry Watterson has said of the suppression of news applies

1. *The Behavior of Crowds* (page 193).

equally to the suppression of individual desire. Neither will suppress. With the normal person, the result of this social suppression is to produce an individual who conforms with sufficient closeness to the standards of his group to enable him to remain comfortably within it.

The tendency, however, of the instincts and desires which hare thus ruled out of conduct is somehow or other, when the conditions are favorable, to seek some avenue of release and satisfaction. To the individual most of these avenues of release are closed. He cannot, for example, indulge his instinct of pugnacity without running foul of the law. The only release which the individual can have is one which commands, however, briefly, the approval of his fellows. That is why Mr. Martin calls crowd psychology and crowd activity "the result of forces hidden in a personal and unconscious psyche of the members of the crowd, forces which are merely released by social gatherings of a certain sort." The crowd enables the individual to express himself according to his desire and without restraint.

He says further, "Every crowd 'boosts for' itself, gives itself airs, speaks with oracular finality, regards itself as morally superior, and will, so far as it has the power, lord it over every one. Notice how each group and section in society, so far as it permits itself to think as crowd, claims to be 'the people.'"

As an illustration of the boosting principle Mr. Martin points out the readiness of most groups to enter upon conflict of one kind or another with opposing groups. "Nothing so easily catches general attention and grips a crowd as a contest of any kind, " he says. "The crowd unconsciously identifies its members with one or the other competitor. Success enables the winning crowd to 'crow over' the losers. Such an action becomes symbolical, and is utilized by the ego to enhance its feeling of importance. In society this egoism tends to take the form of the desire for dominance." According to Mr. Martin, that is why "...whenever any attempt is being made to secure recruits for a movement or a point of view the leaders intuitively assume and reiterate the certainty of ultimate victory."

Two points which Mr. Martin makes seem to me most important. In the first place, Mr. Martin points out with absolute justice that the crowd-mind is by no means limited to the ignorant. "Any class," he says, "may behave and think as a crowd—in fact, it usually does so in so far as its class interests are concerned." Neither is the crowd mind to be found only when there is a physical agglomeration of people. This fact is important to an understanding of the problems of the public relations counsel, because he must bear in mind always that the readers of advertisements, the recipients of letters, the solitary listener at a radio speech, the reader of the morning newspapers are mysteriously part of the crowd-mind.

When Bergson came to America about a decade ago, men and women flocked to his classes, both the French and English sessions. It was obvious to the observer that numbers of disciples who conscientiously attended the full course of lectures understood almost nothing of what was being said. Their behavior was an instance of the crowd-mind.

Everybody read "Main Street." Each reader in his own study tried to react as a crowd-mind. They felt as they thought they ought to.

Initiation scandals, where the crowd-mind has created a brutality not possible to individuals, take place not only in brotherhoods, among what Mr. Martin calls "the lower classes," but also among well-bred college youths and the fraternal orders of successful business and professional men. A more specific instance is the football game, with its manifestations of the crowd-mind among a selected group of individuals. The Ku Klux Klan has numbered among its violent supporters some of the "best" families of the affected localities.

The crowd is a state of mind which permeates society and its individuals at almost all times. What becomes articulate in times of stress under great excitement is present in the mind of the individual at most times and explains in part why popular opinion is so positive and so intolerant of contrary points of view. The college professor in his study on a peaceful summer day is just as likely to be reacting as a unit of crowd-mind, as any member of a lynching party in Texas or Georgia.

Mr. Trotter in his book, *Instincts of the Herd in Peace and War*,[2] gives us further material for study. He discusses the underlying causes and results of "herd" tendencies, stressing the herd's cohesiveness.

The tendency the group has to standardize the habits of individuals and to assign logical reasons for them is an important factor in the work of the public relations counsel. The predominant point of view, according to Mr. Trotter, which translates a rationalized point of view into an axiomatic truth, arises and derives its strength from the fact that it enlists herd support for the point of view of the individual. This explains why it is so easy to popularize many ideas.

"The cardinal quality of the herd is the homogeneity."[3] The biological significance of homogeneity lies in its survival value. The wolf pack is many times as strong as the combined strength of each of its individual members. These results of

---

2. W. Trotter, *"Instincts of the Herd in Peace and War."*

3. It should be explained at the very outset that Mr. Trotter does not use the term "herd" in any derogatory sense. He approaches the entire subject from the point of view of the biologist and compares the gregarious instinct in man to the same instinct in lower forms of life.

homogeneity have created the "herd" point of view.

One of the psychological results of homogeneity is the fact that physical loneliness is a real terror to the gregarious animal, and that association with the herd causes a feeling of security. In man this fear of loneliness creates a desire for identification with the herd in matters of opinion.

It is here, says Mr. Trotter,[4] that we find "the ineradicable impulse mankind has always displayed towards segregation into classes. Each one of us in his opinions and his conduct, in matters of amusement, religion, and politics, is compelled to obtain the support of a class, of a herd within the herd."

Says Mr. Trotter:[5] "The effect of it will clearly be to make acceptable those suggestions which come from the herd, and those only. It is of especial importance to note that this suggestibility is not general, and it is only herd suggestions which are rendered acceptable by the action of instinct, and man is, for example, notoriously insensitive to the suggestions of experience. The history of what is rather grandiosity called human progress everywhere illustrates this. If we look back upon the developments of some such thing as the steam engine, we cannot fail to be struck by the extreme obviousness of each advance, and how obstinately it was refused assimilation until the machine almost invented itself."

The workings of the gregarious instinct in man result frequently in conduct of the most remarkable complexity, but it is characterized by all of the qualities of instinctive action. Such conduct is usually rationalized, but this does not conceal its real character.

We may sincerely think that we vote the Republican ticket because we have thought out the issues of the political cam-

---

4. *Instincts of the Herd in Peace and War* (page 32).
5. *Ibid.*

paign and reached our decision in the cold-blooded exercise of judgment. The fact remains that it is just as likely that we voted the Republican ticket because we did so the year before or because the Republican platform contains a declaration of principle, no matter how vague, which awakens profound emotional response in us, or because our neighbor whom we do not like happens to be a Democrat.

Mr. Lippmann remarks:[6] "For the most part we do not first see and then define, we define first and then see. In the great booming, buzzing confusion of the outer world we pick out of the clutter what is already defined for us, and we tend to perceive that which we have picked out in the form stereotyped for us by our culture."

Mr. Trotter cites as a few of the examples of rationalization the mechanism which "enables the European lady who wears rings in her ears to smile at the barbarism of the colored lady who wears her rings in her nose"[7] and the process which enables Englishman "who is amused by the African chieftain's regard for the top hat as an essential piece of the furniture of state to ignore the identity of his own behavior when he goes to church beneath the same tremendous ensign."

The gregarious tendency in man, according to Mr. Trotter, results in five characteristics which he displays in common with all gregarious animals.

1. *"He is intolerant and fearful of solitude, physical and mental."*[8] The same urge which drives the buffalo into the herd and man into the city requires on the part of the latter a sense of

---

6. *Public Opinion* (page 81).
7. *Instincts of the Herd in Peace and War* (page 38).
8. *Ibid.* (page 112 *et seq*). Italics mine.

spiritual identification with the herd. Man is never so much at home as when on the band wagon.

2. *"He is more sensitive to the voice of the herd than to any other influence."* Mr. Trotter illustrates this characteristic in a paragraph which is worth quoting in its entirety. He says: "It (the voice of the herd) can inhibit or stimulate his thought and conduct. It is the source of his moral codes, of the sanctions of his ethics and philosophy. It can endow him with energy, courage, and endurance, and can as easily take these away. It can make him acquiesce in his own punishment and embrace his executioner, submit to poverty, bow to tyranny, and sink without complaint under starvation. Not merely can it make him accept hardship and suffering unresistingly, but it can make him accept as truth the explanation that his perfectly preventable afflictions are sublimely just and gentle. It is this acme of the power of herd suggestion that is perhaps the most absolutely incontestable proof of the profoundly gregarious nature of man."

3. *"He is subject to the passions of the pack in his mob violence and the passions of the herd in his panics."*

4. *"He is reasonably susceptible to leadership."* Mr. Trotter points out that the need for leadership is often satisfied by leadership of a quality which cannot stand analysis, and which must therefore satisfy some impulse rather than the demands of reason.

5. *"His relations with his fellows are dependent upon the recognition of him as a member of the herd."*

The gregarious tendency, Mr. Trotter believes, is biologically fundamental. He finds therefore that the herd reaction is not confined to outbreaks such as panics and mob violence, but that it is a constant factor in all human thinking and feeling. Discussing the results of the sensitiveness of the individual to the herd point of view, Mr. Trotter says in part, "To believe must be an ineradicable natural bias of man, or in other words, an affirmation, positive or negative, is more readily accepted than rejected, unless its source is definitely dissociated from the herd. *Man is not, therefore suggestible by fits and starts, not merely in panics and mobs, under hypnosis, and so forth, but always, everywhere, and under any circumstances.*"

The suggestibility of people to ideas which are part of the standards of their groups could not be more succinctly expressed than in the old command, "When in Rome do as the Romans."

Psychologists have defined for the public relations counsel the fundamental equipment of the individual mind and its relation to group reactions. We have seen the motivations of the individual mind—the motivations of the group mind. We have seen the characteristics in thought and action of the individual and the group. All these things we have touched on, though briefly, since they form the ground-work of knowledge for the public relations counsel. Their application will be discussed later.

CHAPTER VI

THE GROUP AND HERD ARE THE BASIC MECHANISMS OF PUBLIC CHANGE

The institutions that make public opinion carry on against a background which is in itself a controlling factor. The real character of this controlling background we shall take up later. Let us first consider some examples that prove its existence—then we can look into its origin and its standards.

Powerful standards control the very institutions which are supposed to help form public opinion. It is necessary to understand the origin, the working and the strength of these institutions in order to understand the institutions themselves and their effect upon the public.

In tracing the interaction of institution upon public and public upon institution, one finds a circle of obedience and leadership. The press, the school and other leaders of thought are themselves working in a background which they cannot entirely control.

Let us turn to the press again for a text.

That the press is so frequently unable to achieve a result on which its combined members are unanimously set makes it evident that the press itself is working in a medium which it cannot entirely control. The *New York Times* motto, "All the news that's fit to print," drives this point home. The standards of fitness created in the minds of the publishers express the point of view of a mass of readers, and this enables the newspapers to achieve and maintain circulation and financial success.

The very fact that newspapers must sell to the public is an evidence that they must please the public and in a measure obey it. In the press there is a very human tendency to compromise between giving the public what it wants and giving the public what it *should* want. This is equally true in music, where artists like McCormack or Rachmaninoff popularize their programs. It is true in the drama, where managers, producers and authors combine to adjust plots, situations and endings to what the public will be willing to pay to see. It is true in art, in architecture, in motion pictures. It is true of the lecture platform and of the pulpit.

So-called radical preachers, for example, usually succeed in broadcasting their radical ideas only when their following is prepared to accept their views. The Rev. Percy Stickney Grant was a great problem to the upholders of the accepted order, only because there was so large a body of parishioners eager to hear and accept his *dicta*. The Rev. Billy Sunday, evangelist, derived his following from among people who were awaiting a faith-stirring appeal.

Another evidence of the fact that a powerful outside influence helps make the forces that mould public opinion is shown by the newspapers in the actual selection of news. The public actually demands that certain types of facts be omitted. The standing problem of every newspaper office—the winnowing of the day's news from the mass of material that reaches the editorial desks—illustrates pointedly the need there is to examine the reasons which prompt the editors in selection.

In an exceedingly interesting advertisement published by

the *New York Tribune,* on April 19, 1922, the *Tribune's* editors state the problem most graphically. The advertisement is headed, "What Else Happened That Day?" and it reads as follows:

"Madame Caillaux was on trial in Paris for killing Gaston Calmette.

"In Long Island a woman was mysteriously shot in a doctor's office while on a night visit.

"Forty-five stage coaches were held up in Yellowstone Park by two masked bandits who took all the cash of the 165 tourists.

"Romantic crime, mystery crime, adventurous crime, a public eagerly interested—and they suddenly dropped from the newspapers. The public forgot them. As news, these events became as if they had never happened. Something else had happened.

"The day of Madame Caillaux's acquittal Austria declared war on Serbia. Russia mobilized fourteen army corps on the German border and the price of wheat in this country soared.

"All the news that a newspaper prints is affected by what else happened that day. If an earthquake occurs the day you announce your daughter's engagement her picture may be left out of the newspaper.

"The man who made a golf hole in one the day of the Depsey-Carpentier fight was out of luck so far as an item on the sporting page was concerned.

"When real estate news breaks, semi-news must go. When real news is scarce, semi-news returns to the front page. A very great man picked out Sunday night to dine at a Bowery mission. Monday is usually

a dull day for news, although some big events, notably the sinking of the *Titanic*, came over the wires
Sunday night.

All papers features big news. When there is no
big news, real editing is needed to select the real news
form the semi-news.

"What you read on dull news days is what fixes
your opinion of your country and of your compa-
triots. It is from the non-sensational news that you
see the world and assess, rightly or wrongly, the true
value of persons and events.

"The relative importance your newspaper gives
to an occurrence affects your thought, your character,
and your children's thought and character. For few
daily habits are as firmly established as the habit of
reading the newspaper."

Now each of the items mentioned in the *Tribune's* advertisement was news. Comparison of the newspapers of that
day will undoubtedly show a wide divergence in the manner
in which these items were treated and in the relative importance assigned to each. The basis of the selection was clearly
the general standard of the clientele of each individual appear.

And this selection of ideas for presentation goes on every
medium of thought communication.

This basis of selection has long been recognized. Thus an
article in the *Atlantic Monthly* for February, 1911, Professor
Hargar, formerly head of the Department of Journalism at the
University of Kansas, draws attention to it in regard to newspapers, and points out that "the province of the city paper is
one of news selection.[1] Out of the vast skein of the day's hap-

---

1. Blyer, *The Profession of Journalism* (page 269).

penings what shall it select? More 'copy' is thrown away than is used. The *New York Sun* is written as definitely for a given constituency as is a technical journal. Out of the day's news it gives prominence to that which fits into its scheme of treatment, and there is so much news that it can fill its columns with interesting materials, yet leave untouched a myriad of events. The *New York Evening Post* appeals to another constituency, and is made accordingly. The *World* and the *Journal* have a far different plan, and 'play up' stories that are mentioned briefly, or ignored, by some of their contemporaries. So the writer on the metropolitan paper is trained to sift news, to choose from his wealth of material that which the paper's traditions demand shall receive attention; and so abundant is the supply that he can easily set a feast without exhausting the market's offering. Unconsciously he becomes an epicure, and knows no day will dawn without bringing him his opportunity."

Mr. Lippmann makes the same observation. He says:[2] "Every newspaper when it reaches the reader is the result of a whole series of selections as to what items shall be printed, in what position they shall be printed, how much space each shall occupy, what emphasis each shall have. There are no objective standards here. There are conventions. Take two newspapers published in the same city on the same morning. The headline of one reads: 'Britain pledges aid to Berlin against French Aggression. France Openly Backs Poles.' The headline of the second is: 'Mrs. Stillman's Other Love.' Which you prefer is a matter of taste, but *not entirely a matter of the editor's taste.* It is a matter of his *judgment as to what will absorb the half hour's attention a certain set of readers will give to his newspaper.*"

---

1. *Public Opinion* (page 354).

The American stage continually bows to public demand and consciously ascribes to the public the changes it undergoes. The character of advertising has definitely yielded to public demand and fake advertising has been to a great extent eliminated. Motion pictures have responded, too, to public taste and public pressure, both as to the kind of picture presented and, in isolated instances, to the type of action permitted to appear.

It is therefore apparent that these and the other institutions which modify public opinion carry on against a background which is also in itself a controlling factor. What the real character of this controlling background is we shall now consider.

CHAPTER VII

THE APPLICATION OF THESE PRINCIPLES

Both Trotter, Martin and the other writers we have quoted confirm what the actual experience of the public relations counsel shows—that the cause he represents must have some group reaction and tradition in common with the public he is trying to reach. This must exist before they can react sympathetically upon one another. Given these common fundamentals, much can be done to capitalize or destroy them. It is as untrue to contend that public opinion is manufactured as it is to contend that public opinion governs the agencies which mould it.

The public relations counsel must continually realize that there are always these limitations to his effectiveness.

The very "leaders," men who have been selected from the mass to "lead the nation," live with their ears to the ground for every slight rumbling of public sentiment. Preachers, acknowledged to be the ethical leaders of their flocks, express obedience to public opinion.

The critics who hold these extreme points of view about public opinion have too easily confused cause and effect. The sympathy between the orator and his audience is not one which the orator can create. He can intensify it, or by tactless speaking he can dissipate it, but he cannot manufacture it from thin air.

Margaret Sanger, a leader in the fight for education on birth control, will evoke enthusiasm when she addresses an audience that approves of her sentiments. When, however, she injects her point of view into groups that have a preconceived aversion to them, she is in danger of abuse, if not of actual physical violence. Likewise, a man who would talk of prison reform at a time when the public is aroused by an unwonted crime wave will find little response. On the other hand, when Madam Curie, co-discoverer of radium, came to America, she found a country that was prepared to meet her because of intensive effort on the part of a large radium corporation and a committee of women formed by Marie B. Meloney, to apprise the public of the importance of her visit. Had she come two years sooner, she might have been ignored save by a few scientists.

A historic incident illustrative of the interaction between a leader and a public is that of the sudden turn in the affairs of Rear Admiral Dewey. The idol of the Spanish American War, he nevertheless alienated popular affection by giving to his wife a house which had been presented to him by an admiring public. For some reason the public failed to sympathize with Admiral Dewey's own undoubtedly sound and worthy reasons.

To say, therefore, as some persons have said at great length and with considerable vehemence, that the public relations counsel is responsible for public opinion, is not true. The public relations counsel is not needed to persuade people to standardize their points of view or to persist in their established beliefs. The established point of view becomes established by satisfying some real or assumed human need.

In common with the scenario writer, the preacher, the statesman, the dramatist, the public relations counsel, has his share in making up the mind of the public. The public quite as truly makes up the mind of the journalist, the pamphleteer, the scenario writer, the preacher and the statesman. The main direction of the public mind is often irrevocably set for its leaders.

Hendrik Van Loon, in his "Story of Mankind," paints a picture of the action and interaction between Napoleon the Great and his public in a way that might well have been made to illustrate our point. When Napoleon led the public truly in the direction toward which it was headed, that is, towards democracy and equality, he was its successful leader and its idol, says Van Loon. When in the latter part of his career he turned back to a goal which the public had discarded and was eager to forget, that is, Bourbaonism, Napoleon met with irresistible defeat.

"Damaged Goods" was able to make the American public accept the word "syphilis" because the counsel on public relations projected the doctrine of sex hygiene through those groups and sections of the public which were prepared to work with him.

Public opinion is the resultant of the interaction between two forces.

This may help us to see with greater clarity the position the public relations counsel holds in relation to the world at large, and what the factors are with which he is concerned and by which he accomplishes his work.

We have given somewhat elaborately into the fundamental equipment of the individual mind and its relation to the group mind because the public relations counsel in his work in these fields must constantly call upon his knowledge of individual and group psychology. The public relations counsel can come forward, first, as the representative of established things when their security is shaken, or when they desire greater power; and second, as the representative of the group which is struggling to establish itself.

Mr. Lippmann says propaganda is dependent upon censorship. From my point of view the precise reverse is more nearly true. Propaganda is a purposeful, directed effort to overcome censorship—the censorship of the group mind and the herd reaction.

The average citizen is the world's most efficient censor. His own mind is the greatest barrier between him and the facts. His own "logical proof compartments," his own absolutism are the obstacles which prevent him from seeing in terms of experience and thought rather than in terms of group reaction.

The training of the public relations counsel permits him to step out of his own group to look at a particular problem with the eyes of an impartial observer and to utilize his knowledge of the individual and the group mind to project his clients' point of view.

PART III

TECHNIQUE AND METHOD

CHAPTER I

THE PUBLIC CAN BE REACHED ONLY
THROUGH ESTABLISHED MEDIUMS OF
COMMUNICATION

When the United States was made up of small social units with common traditions and a small geographic and social area, it was comparatively simple for the proponent of a point of view to address his public directly. If he represented a social or a political idea, he could, at no very great expense and with no very great difficulty in the early Eighteenth Century, cover New England with his pamphlets. He could arouse the thirteen colonies with his journals and brochures. That was because the heritage of these groups made them sensitive to the same stimuli. One man, remarks Mr. Lippmann, then was able single-handed to crystallize the common will of his country in his day and generation. Today the greatest superman as yet developed by humanity could not accomplish the same result with the United States.

Populations have increased. In this country geographical areas have increased. Heterogeneity has also increased. A group living in any given area is now extremely likely to have no common ancestry, no common tradition, as such, and no cohesive intelligence. All these elements make it necessary today for the proponent of a point of view to engage an ex-

CRYSTALLIZING PUBLIC OPINION

pert to represent him before society, an expert who must know how to reach groups totally dissimilar as to ideals, customs and even language. It is this necessity which has resulted in the development of the counsel on public relations.

Now it must be understood that the proponent of a point of view, whether acting alone or under the guidance of public relations counsel, must utilize existing avenues of approach. Modern conditions are such that it is not feasible to build up independent organs. Innovators and innovations cannot create their own channels of communication. They must for a great part work through the existing daily press, the existing magazine, the existing lecture circuit, existing advertising mediums, the existing motion picture channels and other means for the communication of ideas. The public relations counsel, on behalf of the groups he represents, must reach majorities and minorities through their respective approaches.

If the public relations counsel can succeed in presenting ideas and facts to the public in spite of the heterogeneity of society, in spite of the vast psychological and geographic problems, in spite of the difficulties, monetary and otherwise, of reaching and influencing populations numbering millions—if he can succeed in overcoming these difficulties by a skillful understanding of the situation, his profession is socially valuable.

Absolute homogeneity, resulting in a dead level of uniformity in public and individual reaction, is undesirable. On the other hand, agreement on broad social purposes is essential to progress. Agreement on broad industrial purposes may be equally desirable. Without such agreement, without unified purposes, there can be no progress and the unit must fall. The men who were most effective in stimulating national morale during the war never lost sight of these underlying needs, whether they stimulated a whole nation to ration itself voluntarily and give up the eating of sugar, or whether they stimulated knitting and Red Cross activities and voluntary contributions to funds.

Three ways are cited by Mr. Lippmann to obtain cohesive force among the special and local interests which make up national and social units. The public relations counsel avails himself only of the third. The first method which is described is that of "patronage and pork." This is very largely the method relied upon by certain legislative bodies today to maintain cohesive force. As an instance of this, the investigations of the methods used in connection with the bills to secure the building of local post offices or the dredging of harbors or rivers seem to point out that a representative from one community will promise reciprocal support to the member from another community, if he in turn will act favorably on another item. This method intensifies the feeling that all are working together, even though they may not be working for the highest interests of the country. Similarly the chief executive of a city may institute certain measures to placate school teachers. He will expect the school teachers to support him on some other project at some other period.

The second method named by Mr. Lippmann[1] is "government by terror and obedience."

The third method is "government based on such highly developed system of information, analysis and self-consciousness that the 'knowledge of national circumstances and reasons of state' is evident to all men. The autocratic system is in decay. The voluntary system is in its very earliest development and so, in calculating the prospects of associations among large groups of people, a league of nations, industrial govern-

1. *Public Opinion* (page 292).

ment, or a federal union of states, the degree to which the material for a common consciousness exists determines how far cooperation will depend upon force, or upon the milder alternative to force, which is patronage and privilege. The secret of great state builders, like Alexander Hamilton, is that they know how to calculate these principles."

The method of education by information, which was to a great extent relied upon by the United States, for example, was evidenced in the formation during the war of such agencies as the Committee on Public Information. The public relations counsel, through the mediums chosen by him, presented to the public the information necessary to aid in understanding America's war aims and ideals. George Creel and his organization reached vast groups, representing every phase of our national elements, in every modern method of thought communication. But even in the United States the other two methods were used to obtain cohesive force.

In fact the method least relied upon in any of the belligerent countries was that of "government based on such a highly developed system of information, analysis and self-consciousness that 'the knowledge of national circumstances and reasons of state' is evident to all men."

This breakdown did not occur among small, inefficiently organized groups. It occurred among the representatives of the highest development in social organizations.

If this was the fate of the most highly organized social groups, consider then the problem which confronts the social, economic, educational or political groups in peace time, when they attempt to obtain a public hearing for new ideas. Innumerable instances have shown the difficulty that any group faces in gaining an acceptance for its ideas.

The development of the United States to its present size

and diversification has intensified the difficulty of creating a common will on any subject because it has heightened the natural tendency of men to separate into crowds opposed to one another in point of view. This difficulty is further emphasized by the fact that often these crowds live in different traditional, moral and spiritual worlds. The physical difficulties of communication make group separation greater.

Mr. Trotter's conclusions from a study of the gregarious instinct are singularly apt on this point. He says that[2] "the enormous power of varied reaction possessed by man must render necessary for his attainment of the full advantages of the gregarious habit a power of inter-communication of absolutely unprecedented fineness. It is clear that scarcely a hint of such power has yet appeared, and it is equally obvious that it is this defect which gives to society the characteristics which are the contempt of the man of science and the disgust of the humanitarian."

When the worker was of the same ancestry as his employer, labor difficulties, for example, could be discussed in terms which were comprehensible to both parties. Today the United States Steel Corporation must exert tremendous effort to present its view to its thousands of employees who are South Europeans, North Europeans, Americans.

Czechoslovakia, during the Peace Conferences, wanted to appeal to its countrymen in America, but this group was vague and scattered in a population that lived in many cities throughout the country. The public relations counsel who was engaged to reach this scattered population had, therefore, to translate his appeals so that they might be understood logically and emotionally by the educated and the uneducated, the urban, the rural, the laboring and the professional man.

---

2. *Instincts of the Herd in Peace and War* (page 62).

The same problem in quite a different guise presented itself to the public relations counsel who wanted to insure a public response to the appeal of the Diaghileff Russian Ballet, of which the public knew nothing. He had, therefore, to surmount the difficulties of dissimilar geographic and artistic heritage and taste, of unwillingness to accept novelty and of interests already firmly attached to other forms of amusement.

Dominant groups today are more secure in their position than was the most successful autocrats of several hundred years ago, because today the inertia which must be overcome in order to displace these groups is so much greater. So many persons with so many different points of view must be reached and unified before anything effective can be done. Unity can be secured only by finding the greatest common factor or divisor of all the groups; and it is difficult to find one common factor which will appeal to a large and unhomogeneous group.

A very simple and broodingly appealing campaign for reaching the public was undertaken recently by the railroads in combination. They utilized the poster in graphic, fundamental appeal to awaken an instinct of carefulness in regard to crossing railroad tracks. When the government sought to reestablish ex-service men, the public relations counsel had to appeal vividly and quickly to employers and returned soldiers out of the vast complexity of their interests. He selected the most fundamental appeals of loyalty, fairness and patriotism in order to be understood actively.

Domination today is not a product of armies or navies or wealth or policies. It is a domination based on the one hand upon accomplished unity, and on the other hand upon the fact that opposition is generally characterized by a high degree of disunity. The institution of electing representatives to Congress is so firmly established that no existent force today can overthrow it. More specifically, why is it that the two parties, Republican and Democrat, have maintained themselves as the dominant force for so many years? Only the leadership of Theodore Roosevelt seemed for a time to supersede them; and events since then have shown that it was Roosevelt and not his party who succeeded. The Farmer-Labor Party, the Socialist Party despite years of campaigning have failed to become even strongly recognizable opponents to the established groups. The disunity of forces which seek to overthrow dominant groups is illustrated every day in every phase of our lives—political, moral and economic. A new point of view, although faced by the difficulty of unifying a group to concerted will or action, can seldom establish new mediums by which to approach those people to whom it wishes to appeal.

It is possible for advertising and pamphletizing to blanket the country at a cost. To establish a new lecture service in order to reach the public would be expensive, and effective only to a limited extent. To establish an independent radio station to broadcast an idea would be difficult and probably disproportionately expensive. To create a new motion picture and a distributing agency would be slow, and very difficult and costly, if possible at all.

The difficulty of establishing and building new channels of approach to the public is shown best by an examination of the principal mediums which are available to the public relations counsel who desires to direct public thought to the problems of the group he represents.

It is only necessary to picture the newspaper and magazine situation in the United States today to realize the difficulty of establishing a new medium for the representation of a point of view. Americans are accustomed to first-rate service from their press. They demand a high standard not only in the physical appearance of their newspapers but in the news service as well. Their daily paper must provide them with items of local, state and international interest and importance. In the complex activities of modern life, the newspaper must find and select the subjects which interest its readers. It must also give to its readers the news fresh from the making. Whatever vagueness there may be about the definition of news itself, one admitted constant is that it must be fresh.

The cost of establishing a paper with a wide appeal, which will have the facilities of gathering news, of printing and distributing it, is such that groups can no longer depend upon their own organs of expression. The Christian Science church does not depend upon its admirable publication, the *Christian Science Monitor* in order to reach its own and new publics. Even where the issue demands a partisan or class origin of a newspaper, as in the case of a political party, the results achieved by so expensive and laborious a step seldom justify it.

Mr. Given in his book *Making a Newspaper*, points out the great expense that is attached to the publication of a large metropolitan daily. In proportion to their field of appeal and potential income, the smaller dailies undoubtedly face the same economic problems. Mr. Given says:[3] "Few persons not having intimate knowledge of a newspaper have any idea of the great amount of money required to start one, or to keep one running which is already established. The mechanical equipment and delivery service alone may demand an investment of several hundred thousand dollars—there is one New York paper whose mechanical equipment cost $1,000,000— supplies are in constant demand, and the salary list is a long and heavy one. For a new paper the salary list of the editorial

---

3.Given, *Making a Newspaper* (pages 306-307).

department is especially formidable, as editors and reporters who have employment with well-established publications are always reluctant to change to a venture that at best is in for a rough voyage, and can be attracted only by high pay.

"A good many of the newspapers that are started soon become memories, and fewer than are generally supposed are paying their own way. The sum of $3,000,000 would hardly suffice at the present time to equip a first-class newspaper establishment in New York City, issue a morning and an evening edition paper, build up a circulation of 75,000 for each, and place the establishment on a money-making basis. Run on the lines of those already established and possessing no extraordinary features to recommend them to the public, the two papers might continue to lose money for twenty years. When one learns that there are in New York business managers who are compelled to reckon with an average weekly expense account of nearly $50,000, he can understand the possibility of heavy losses. And it might be added, in contrast, that there are in New York newspapers which could not be bought for $10,000,000."

Discussing substantially the same point, Mr. Oswald Garrison Villard observes the narrowing down of the number of newspapers in our large cities and points out the imminent danger of a news monopoly in the United States. He says:[4] "It is the danger that newspaper conditions, because of the enormously increased costs and this tendency to monopoly, may prevent people who are actuated by passion and sentiment from founding newspapers, which is causing many students of the situation much concern. What is to be the hope for the

---

4. "Press Tendencies and Dangers," *Atlantic Monthly*, January, 1918.

advocates of newborn and unpopular reforms if they cannot have a press of their own, as the Abolitionists and the founders of the Republican party set up theirs in a remarkably short time, usually with poverty-stricken bank accounts?"

The public relations counsel must always subdivide the appeal of his subject and present it through the widest possible variety of avenues to the public. That these avenues must be existing avenues is both a limitation and an opportunity.

People accept the facts which come to them through existing channels. They like to hear new things in accustomed ways. They have neither the time nor the inclination to search for facts that are not readily available to them. The expert, therefore, must advise first upon the form of action desirable for his client and secondly must utilize the established mediums of communication, in order to present to the public a point of view. This is true whether it is that of a majority or minority, old or new personality, institutions or group which desires to change by modification or intensification the store of knowledge and the opinion of the public.

CHAPTER II

THE INTERLAPPING GROUP FORMATIONS OF SOCIETY, THE CONTINUOUS SHIFTING OF GROUPS, CHANGING CONDITIONS AND THE FLEXIBILITY OF HUMAN NATURE ARE ALL AIDS TO THE COUNSEL ON PUBLIC RELATIONS

The public relations counsel works with public opinion. Public opinion is the product of individual minds. Individual minds make up the group mind. And the established order of things is maintained by the inertia of the group. Three factors make it possible for the public relations counsel to overcome even this inertia. These are, first, the interlapping group formation of society; second, the continuous shifting of groups; third, the changed physical conditions to which groups respond. All of these are brought about by the natural inherent flexibility of individual human nature.

Society is not divided into two groups, although it seems so to many. Some see modern society divided into capital and labor. The feminist sees the world divided into men and women. The hungry man sees the rich and the por. The missionary sees the heathen and the faithful. If society were divided into two groups, and no more, then change could come about only through violent upheaval.

Let us assume, for example, a society divided into capital

and labor. It is apparent on slight inspection that capital is not a homogenous group. There is a difference in point of view and in interests between Elbert H. Gary or John D. Rockefeller, Jr., on the one hand, and the small shopkeeper on the other.

Occasions arise, too, upon which even in one group sharp differences and competitive alignments take place.

In the capital group, on the tariff question, for example, the retailer with a net income of ten thousand dollars a year is apt to take a radically different position from the manufacturer with a similar income. In some respects the capitalist is a consumer. In other respects he is a worker. Many persons are at the same time workers and capitalists. The highly paid worker who also draws income from Liberty Bonds or from shares of stock in industrial corporations is an example of this.

On the other hand, the so-called workers do not consist of a homogenous group with complete identity of interests. There may be no difference in economic situation between manual labor and mental labor; yet there is a traditional difference in point of view which keeps these two groups far apart. Again, the narrower the field of manual labor, the group represented by the American Federation of Labor, is frequently opposed in sympathies and interests to the group of Industrial Workers of the World. Even in the American Federation of Labor there are component units. The locomotive engineer, who belongs to one of the great brotherhoods, has different interests from the miner, who belongs to the United Mine Workers of America.

The farmer is in a class by himself. Yet he in turn may be a tenant farmer or the owner of an estate or of a small patch of tillable soil.

That group so vaguely called "the public" consists of all

sorts and conditions of men, the particular kind or condition depending upon the point of view of the individual who is making the observation or classification. This is true likewise of great and small subdivisions of the public.

The public relations counsel must take into account that many groups exist, and that there is a very definite interlapping of groups. Because of this he is enabled to utilize many types of appeal in reaching any one group, which he subdivides for his purposes.

The Federation for the Support of Jewish Charities recently instituted a campaign to raise millions of dollars for what it called its United Building Fund. The directors of that campaign might have subdivided society for their purpose into two groups, the Jewish and the non-Jewish group, or they might have decided that there were rich people who could give and poor people who could not give. But they realized the interlapping nature of the groups they wanted to reach. They analyzed these component groups closely and divided them into groups which had common business interests. For instance, they organized a group of dentists, a group of bankers, a group of real estate operators, a group of cloak-and-suit-house operators, a group of motion picture and theatrical owners and others.

Through an approach to each group on the strongest appeal to which the members of the group as a group would respond, the charity received the support of the individuals who made it up. The social aspirations of the group, the ambitions for leadership of the group, the ambitions for leadership of the group, the competitive desires and philanthropic tendencies of the individuals who made up these groups were capitalized.

The interlapping nature of these groups made it possible, too, for the public relations counsel to reach all the individuals by appeals that were directed not merely to the individual as a member of the business group with which he was aligned, but also as a member of a different group. For instance, as a humanitarian, as a public-spirited citizen, or as a devoted Jew. Because of this interlapping characteristic of groups, the organization was able to accomplish its purpose more successfully.

Society is made up of an almost infinite number of groups, whose various interests and desires overlap and interweave inextricably. The same man may be at the same time the member of a minority religious sect, supporter of the dominant political party, a worker in the sense that he earns his living primarily by his labor, and a capitalist in the sense that he has rents from real estate investments or interest from financial investments. In an issue which involves his religious sect he will align himself with one group. In an issue which involves the choice of a President of the United States he aligns himself with another group. In an individual issue between capital and labor it might be very nearly impossible to estimate in advance how he would align himself. It is from the constant interplay of these groups and of their conflicting interests upon each other that progress results, and it is this fact that the public relations counsel takes into account in pleading his cause. A movement called "The Go-Getters," instituted by a magazine as much as to keep itself before the public eye as to stimulate commercial activity, found rapid acceptance throughout the country because it appealed to trades of every description, because each group had among is members men who belonged also to a large group, the group of salesmen.

Let us examine for a moment the personnel of the Horseshoe at the Metropolitan Opera House. It is comprised of people who are rich, but this economic classification is only one, for the men and women who assemble there are presumably music lovers. But we may again break up this classification of music lovers and discover that this group contains art lovers as well. It contains sportsmen. It contains merchants and bankers. There are philosophers in it. There are motorists and amateur farmers. When the Russian Ballet came to America the essential parts of this group attended the performances, but in going after his public, the public relations counsel based his actions upon the interlapping of groups, and appealed to his entire possible audience through their various interlapping group interests. The art lover had been stimulated by hearing of the Ballet through his art group or the art publications and by seeing pictures of the costumes and the settings. The music lover, who might have had his interest stimulated through seeing a photograph, also had his interest stimulated by reading about the music.

Every individual heard of the Russian Ballet in terms of one or more different appeals and responded to the Ballet because of these appeals. It is naturally difficult to say which one of them had its strongest effect upon the individual's mind. There was no doubt, however, that the interlapping group formation of society made it possible for more to be reached and to be moved than would have been the case if the Ballet had been projected on the world at large only as a well-balanced artistic performance.

The utilization of this characteristic of society was shown recently in the activities of a silk firm which desired to intensify the interest of the public in silks. It realized that fundamentally women were its potential buying public, but it understood, too, that the women who made up this public were members of other groups as well. Thus, to the members of women's clubs, silk was projected as the embodiment of fashion. To those women who visited museums, silk was displayed there as art. To the schools in the same town, perhaps, silk became a lesson in the natural history of the silkworm. To art clubs, silk became color and design. To newspapers, the events that transpired in the silk mills became news matters of importance.

Each group of women was appealed to on the basis of its greatest interest. The school teacher was appealed to in the schoolroom as an educator, and after school hours as a member of a women's club. She read the advertisements about silk as a woman reader of the newspapers, and as a member of the women's group which visited the museums, saw the silk there. The woman who stayed at home was brought into contact with the silk through her child. All these groups made up the potential market for silk, reached in this way in terms of many appeals to each individual. These are the implications present for the public relations counsel, who must take into account the interchange and interplay of groups in pleading his cause.

For society, the interesting outcome of this situation is that progress seldom occurs through the abrupt expulsion by a group of its old ideas in favor of new ideas, but rather through the rearrangement of the thought of the individuals in these groups with respect to each other and with respect to the entire membership of society.

It is precisely this interlapping of groups—the variety, the inconsistency of the average man's mental, social and psychological commitments which makes possible the gradual change from one state of affairs or from one state of mind to another. Few people are life members of one group and of one group only. The ordinary person is a very temporary member of a great number of groups. This is one of the most powerful forces making for progress in society because it makes for receptivity and open-mindedness. The modification which results from the inconstancy of individual commitments may be accelerated and directed by conscious effort. These changes which come about so stealthily that they remain unobserved in society until long after they have taken place, can be made to yield results in chosen directions.

Changed external conditions must be taken into account by the public relations counsel in his work.

Such changes carry with them modifications in the interests and points of view of those they affect. They make it possible to modify group and individual reaction. The public relations counsel, too, can modify the results of the changed external condition by calling attention to it or interpreting it in terms of the interest of those affected.

The radio might be taken as an example. In considering the radio from the standpoint of his work, the public relations counsel has a new medium which can readily reach huge sections of the public with his message. The public relations counsel must be ready to estimate, too, what difference in viewpoint the radio will produce or has produced in any given section of the public it reaches. He will have to consider, for instance, that due to it the average farmer is much more closely in contact with the world's events than formerly.

In the case of the radio, too, if his clients be, for instance, large manufacturers of radio supplies and demand acceleration of this changed external condition in order to increase their business, he may enlarge the radio's field, activity and effectiveness. Or, he may stress to the public the importance of this new instrument and strengthen its prestige, so that it may better fulfill its mission as a modifier of conditions.

Changed conditions can make possible modifications in the public point of view, as can be instanced by a campaign carried on by savings banks to encourage thrift. This campaign was successful at that time because inflation made it easy for the public to see the wisdom of the doctrines preached and to act upon them.

Another example of this modification in the public point of view due to a changed condition was the demand made by the Executive Committee of the Central Trades and Labor Council of New York for the government to take over the railways of the country. Public ownership had been a pet subject for school debate for more than two decades, but it had seldom passed into the field of serious considerations by the general public. Yet the conditions of hardship created by the last strike of the railroad shopmen caused a much greater receptivity in the public mind to this idea.

The airplane slowly emerges as an important factor in the daily life of the people. What it will mean in the psychology of the nation when commuters can settle within a radius of a hundred or more miles of cities is only to be guessed at. Cities may cease to exist except as industrial centers. There will be greater groups and broader interests. There will be fewer geographic divisions.

When the automobile was first used motoring was a dangerous and thrilling sport. Today it is found that the automobile has altered the fundamental conception of daily life held by thousands of people, both in the urban and the rural population. The automobile has removed much of the isolation of country districts. It has increased the possibility of education in them. It has caused millions of miles of excellent roads to be laid.

Changed conditions can be national or local in their important and significance. They can be as national in scope as the revolutionary introduction over night of a national prohibition law or as local as a police captain's edict in Coney Island against stockingless feminine bathers. But they must be taken into consideration by the public relations counsel in his work if they concern in the slightest degree his particular public.

The basic elements of human nature are fixed as to desires and instincts and innate tendencies. The directions, however, in which these basic elements may be turned by skillful handling are infinite. Human nature is readily subject to modifications. Many psychologists have attempted to define the component parts of human nature, and while their terminology is not the same, they do follow more or less the same general outlines.

Among the universal instincts are—self-preservation, which includes the desire for shelter, sex hunger and food hunger. It is only necessary to look through the pages of any magazine to see the way in which modern business avails itself of these three fundamentals to exert a coercive force upon the public it is trying to reach. The American Radiator advertisement with its cozy home, the family gathered around the radiator, the storm raging outside, definitely makes its appeal to the universal desire for shelter.

The Golden Mustard advertisements with their graphic delineation of cold cuts and an inviting glass of what is presumably near-beer definitely appeal to our gustatory sense.

As for the sex appeal, the soap advertisements run a veritable rate with these ends in view. Woodbury's "the skin you love to touch" is such a graphic illustration.

The instinct of self-preservation, one of the most basic of human instincts, is most flexible. The dispensers of raisins, upon the advice of an expert on public opinion, adopted a slogan to appeal to this instinct: "Have you had your iron today?"—iron presumably strengthening a man and increasing his powers of resistance. The same man appealed to here will respond to the sales talk which persuades him that insurance may save him at a time of need.

An important hair-net manufacturer wanted to increase the sales of his product. The public relations counsel, therefore, appealed to the instinct of self-preservation of large groups of the public. He talked of self-preservation with respect to hygiene for food dispensers. He talked of self-preservation with respect to safety for women who work near exposed machinery.

The same instinct of preservation which may cause a worker to give up necessary food so that he may save a little money will cause him to contribute money to a common fund if he can be shown that this too is a safety measure.

The public relations counsel extracts from his clients' causes ideas which will capitalize certain fundamental instincts in the people he is trying to reach, and then sets about to project these ideas to his public.

William McDougall, the psychologist, classifies seven primary instincts with their attendant emotions. They are flight-fear, repulsion-disgust, curiosity-wonder, pugnacity-anger, self-display-elation, self-abasement-subjection, parental-love-tenderness. These instincts are utilized by the pubic relations counsel in developing ideas and emotions which will modify the opinions and actions of his public.

The action of public healthy officials in stressing the possibility of a plague or epidemic is effective because it appeals to the emotion of fear, and presents the possibility of preventing the spread of the epidemic or plague. Of course, the element of flight in this particular situation is not one of movement, but of a desire to get away from the danger.

The instinct of repulsion with its attendant emotion of

disgust is not often called upon by the public relations counsel in his work.

On the other hand, curiosity and wonder are continually employed. In Governmental work, particularly , the statesman who has an announcement to make is continually exhausting every effort to arouse pubic interest in advance of the actual announcement. Feelers are often sent out to the public to help create curiosity.

It is interesting to note, too, that even book publishers rely upon the element of wonder, termed suspense in drama, to increase their public and their sales. Our now famous "What is wrong with this picture?" advertisements, and those used for the O. Henry books illustrate this point.

Pugnacity with its attendant emotion of anger is a human constant. The public relations counsel uses this continually in constructing all kinds of events that will call it into play. Because of it, too, he is often forced to enact combats and create issues. He stages battles against evils in which the antagonist is personified for the public. New York City, when it wants to reduce the death rate from tuberculosis, aligns its citizens yearly in a fight against the disease and continues the idea of combat by announcing the number of victims from year to year. It uses the terminology of warfare in these bulletins. Such phrases in this or other health campaigns as "kill the germ," "swat the fly," illustrate this point. The public responds to a battle in a way that it might not respond to a plea and take care of itself or do its civic duty.

Under pugnacity would come that technique of the public relations counsel which is continually devising tests and contests. Mr. Martin, in his experience as director of the Cooper Union Forum, noticed that the sort of interest which will most easily bring an assemblage of people together is most commonly an issue of some kind.

On the other hand, says Mr. Martin:[1] "I have seen efforts made in New York to hold mass meetings to discuss affairs of the very greatest importance, and I have noted the fact that such efforts usually fail to get out more than a handful of specially interested persons, no matter how well advertised, if the subject to be considered happens not to be of a controversial nature. On the other hand, if the matter to be considered is one about which there is keen partisan feeling and popular resentment—if it lends itself to the spectacular personal achievement of one whose name is known, especially in the face of opposition or difficulties—or if the occasion permits of resolutions of protest, of the airing of wrongs, of denouncing a business of some kind, or of casting statements of external principles in the teeth of 'enemies of humanity,' then, however, trivial the occasion, we may count on it that our meeting will be well attended.

"It is this element of conflict, directly or indirectly, which plays an overwhelming part in the psychology of every crowd. It is the element of contest which makes baseball so popular. A debate will draw a larger crowd than a lecture. One of the secrets of the large attendance of the forum is the fact that discussion—'talking back'—is permitted and encouraged. The Evangelist Sunday undoubtedly owes the great attendance at his meetings in no small degree to the fact that he is regularly expected to abuse some one.

"Nothing so easily catches general attention and creates a crowd as a contest of any kind. The crowd unconsciously identifies its members with one or the other competitor. Success enables the winning crowd to 'crow' over the losers. Such

---

1. *The Behavior of Crowds* (page 23-24).

an occasion becomes symbolic and is utilized by the ego to enhance its feeling of importance."

The public relations counsel finds in the instinct of pugnacity a powerful weapon for enlisting public support for or public opposition to a point of view in which he is interested. On this principle, he will, whenever possible, state his case in the form of an issue and enlist, in support of his side, such forces as are available.

The dangers of the method must be recognized and borne in mind. Pugnacity can be enlisted on the side of decency and progress. He who looks at it from that point of view will agree with Mr. Pulitzer, the great publisher, that it seems neither extraordinary nor culpable, that "people and press should be more interested in the polemical than in the platitudinous; in blame than in painting the lily; in attack than in sending laudatory coals to Newcastle." On the other hand, the instinct of pugnacity can be utilized to suppress and to oppress. From the point of view of the public relations counsel, who is interested from day to day in accomplishing definite results on specific issues, the dangers of the method are only the ordinary dangers of every weapon, physical or psychological, which has been devised.

It is interesting in this connection to note that a newspaper uses the same methods to encourage interest in itself as do others. The *New York Times* promoted public interest in heavier-than-air-machines by creating sporting issues of contest between aviators on altitude records, continuous stays in the air, distance flying and so forth.

Mr. Lippmann comments on this same characteristic:

"But where pugnacity is not enlisted, those of us who are not directly involved find it hard to keep up our interest. For those who are involved the absorption may be real enough to hold them even when no issue is involved. They may be exercised by sheer joy in activity or by subtle rivalry or invention. But for those to whom the whole problem is external and distant, these other faculties do not easily come into play. In order that the faint image of the affair shall mean something to them, they must be allowed to exercise, the love of struggle, suspense and victory."[2]

We have to take sides. We have to be able to take sides. In the recesses of our being we must step out of the audience onto the stage and wrestle as the hero for the victory of good over evil. We must breathe into the allegory the breath of our life.

Recently a philanthropic group was advised to hold a prize fight for charity. This recognition of the importance of the principle of pugnacity was correct. It is a question whether the application was not somewhat ill advised and in bad taste. The Consumer's Committee of Women opposed to American Valuation was avowedly aligned to fight against a section of the tariff presented by Chairman Fordney. The Lucy Stone League, a group who wish to make it easy for married women to maintain their maiden names, dramatized the fight that they are making against tradition by staging a debate at their annual banquet.

Very often the public relations counsel utilizes the self-display-elation motive and draws public attention to particular people in groups, in order to give them a greater interest in the work they are espousing. It is often found to be true that when a man's adherence or allegiance to a movement is lukewarm and he is publicly praised for his adherence to it, he will become a forceful factor in it. That is why the intelligent hospital boards name rooms or beds after their donors. It is one of the reasons for the elaborate letterheads so many of our

2. Walter Lippman, *Public Opinion*.

philanthropic organizations have.

Self-abasement and subjection, its attendant emotion, are seldom called upon. On the other hand, parental love and tenderness are continually employed, viz., the effort of the baby-kissing candidate for public office or the attempt to popularize a brand of silk by having a child present a silk flag to a war veteran at a public ceremony. The whole flood of post-war charity-drives was keyed to this pitch. The starving Belgian orphan personified in every picture, the starving Armenian, and then the hungry Austrian and German orphans appeared, and the campaigns all succeeded on this issue. Even issues where the child was not the predominant factor used this appeal.

Four other instincts are listed in this classification—gregariousness, individualism, acquisition and construction. We have already dealt with the first at length.

The gregarious instinct in man gives the public relations counsel the opportunity for his most potent work. The group and herd show everywhere the leader, who because of certain qualifications, certain points that are judged by the herd to be important to its life, stands out and is followed more or less implicitly by it.

A group leader gains such power with his group or herd that even on mattes which have had nothing to do with the establishment or gaining of that leadership he is considered a leader and is followed by his group.

It is this attribute of men and women that again gives the pubic relations counsel free play.

A group leader of any given cause will bring to a new cause all those who have looked to his leadership. For instance, if the adherence of a prominent Republican is secured for the League of Nations, his adherence will probably bring to the League of Nations many other prominent Republicans.

The group leadership with which the public relations counsel may work is limited only by the character of the groups he desires to reach. After an analysis of his problem the subdivisions must be made. His action depends upon his selective capacity, and the possibility of approach to the leaders. These leaders may represent therefore a wide variety of interests—society leaders or leaders of political groups, leaders of women or leaders of sportsmen, leaders of divisions by geography, or divisions by age, divisions by language or by education. These subdivisions are so numerous that there are large companies in the United States whose business it is to supply lists of groups and group leaders in different fields.

This same mechanism is carried out in many other cases. In looking for group leaders, the public relations counsel must realize that some leaders have more varied and more intensified authority than others. One leader may represent the ideals and ideas of several or numerous groups. His cooperation on one basis may bring into alignment and may carry with it the other groups who are interested in him primarily for other reasons.

The public relations counsel, let us say, enlists the support of a man, president of two associations: (a) an economic association, (b) a welfare association. The issue is an economic one, purely. But because of his leadership, the membership of association (b), that is, the welfare group, joins him in the movement as interestedly as association (a) does, which has the more logical, direct reason for entering the field.

I have given this in general terms rather than as a specific instance. The principle which governs the interlapping and continually shifting group formation of society also governs the gregariousness.

Individualism, another instinct, is a concomitant of gregariousness, and naturally follows it. The desire for individual expression is always a trait of the individuals who go to make up the group. The appeal to individualism goes closely in hand with other instincts, such as self-display.

The instincts of acquisition and construction are minor instincts as far as the ordinary work of the public relations counsel is concerned. Examples of this type of appeal come readily to mind in the "Own your own home" and "Build your own home" campaign.

The innate tendencies are susceptibility to suggestion, imitation, habit and play. Susceptibility to suggestion and imitation might well be classified under gregariousness, which we have already discussed.

Under habit would come one very important human trait of which the public relations counsel avails himself continually. The mechanism which habit produces and which make it possible for the public relations counsel to use habit is the stereotype we have already touched upon.

Mental habits create stereotypes just as physical habits create certain definite reflex actions. These stereotypes or reflex images are a great aid to the public relations counsel in his work.

These short-cuts to reactions make it possible for the average mind to possess a much larger number of impressions than would be possible without them. At the same time these stereotypes or *clichés* are not necessarily truthful pictures of what they are supposed to portray. They are determined by the outward stimuli to which the individual has been subject as well as by the content of his mind.

To most of us, for example, the stereotype of the general is a stern, upright gentleman in uniform and with gold braid, preferably on a horse. The stereotype of a farm is a slouching, overall-clad man with straw sticking out of his mouth and a straw hat on his head. He is supposed to be very shrewd when it comes to matters of his own farm and very ignorant when it comes to matters of culture. He despises "city fellers." All this is the connotation brought up by the one word "farmer."

The public relations counsel sometimes uses the current stereotypes, sometimes combats them and sometimes creates new ones. In using them he very often brings to the public he is reaching a stereotype they already know, to which he adds his new ideas, thus he fortifies his own and gives a greater carrying power. For instance, the public relations counsel might well advise Austria, which in the public mind still represent a belligerent country, to bring forward other Austrian stereotypes, namely the Danube waltz stereotype and the Danube blue stereotype. An appeal for help would then come from the country of the well-liked Danube waltz and Danube blue—the country of gayety and charm. The new idea would be carried to those who accepted the stereotypes they were familiar with.

The combating of the stereotype is seen in the battle waged against the American Valuation Plan by the public relations counsel. The formulators of the plan dubbed it "American Valuation" in order to capitalize on the stereotype of "American." In fighting the plan, its opponents put the word "American" in quotation marks whenever reference was made to the subject in order to question the authenticity of the use of this stereotype. Thus patriotism was definitely removed from what was evidently an economical and political issue.

The public relations counsel creates new stereotypes. Roosevelt, his own best adviser, was an apt creator of such stereotypes—"square deal, delighted, molly-coddle, big stick," created new concepts for general acceptance.

Stereotypes sometimes becomes shop-worn and lose their power with the public that has previously accepted them. "Hundred per cent American" died from over use.

Visible objects as stereotypes are often used by the public relations counsel with great effectiveness to produce the desired impression. A national flag on the orator's platform is a most common device. A scientist must of necessity be in juxtaposition with his instruments. A chemist is not a chemist to the public unless test tubes and retorts are near him. A doctor must have his kit, or, formerly, a Van Dyke beard. In photographs of food factory buildings white is a good stereotype for cleanliness and purity. In fact, all emblems and trade-makes are stereotypes.

There is one danger in the use of stereotypes by the public relations counsel. That is, by the substitution of words for acts, demagogues in every field of social relationship can take advantage of the public.

Play as an innate tendency is utilized by the public relations counsel whenever conditions merit such an appeal. When a charity committee is advised to institute a street fair to gather money, the committee is recognizing this tendency. When a city government arranges fireworks for it citizens, when a metropolitan newspaper daily stages marble contests or horseshoe pitching events, the play tendency of human society finds an outlet and the imitators of the event find friends.

CHAPTER III

AN OUTLINE OF METHODS PRACTICABLE IN MODIFYING THE POINT OF VIEW OF A GROUP

On the question of specific devices upon which the public relations counsel relies to accomplish his ends, volumes could probably be written without exhausting the subject. The detailed presentation is potentially endless. Pages could be filled with instances of the stimuli to which men and women respond, the circumstances under which they will respond favorably or unfavorably, and the particular application of each of these stimuli to create conditions. Such an outline, however, would have less value than an outline of fundamentals, since circumstances are never the same.

These principles, by and large, consist of fundamentals already defined, to which the public relations counsel has recourse in common with the statesman, the journalist, the preacher, the lecturer, and all others engaged in attempting to modify public opinion or public conduct.

How does the public relations counsel approach any particular problem? First he must analyze his client's problem and his client's objective. Then he must analyze the public he is trying to reach. He must devise a plan of action for the client to follow and determine the methods and the organs of distribution available for reaching his public. Finally he must try to estimate the interaction between the public he seeks to reach and his client. How will his client's case strike the public mind? And by public mind here is meant that section or those sections of the public which must be reached.

Let us take the example of a public relations counsel who is confronted with the specific problem of modifying or influencing the attitude of the public toward a given tariff bill. A tariff bill, of course, is primarily the application of theoretical economics to a concrete industrial situation. The public relations counsel in analyzing must see himself simultaneously as a member of a large number of publics. He must visualize himself as a manufacturer, a retailer, an importer, an employer, a worker, a financier, a politician.

Within these groups he must see himself again as a member of the various subdivisions of each of these groups. He must see himself, for example, as a member of a group of manufacturers who obtain the bulk of their raw material within the United States, and at the same time as a member of a group of manufacturers who obtain large portions of their raw material from abroad and whose importations of raw material may be adversely affected by the pending tariff bill. He must see himself not only as a farm laborer but also as a mechanic in a large industrial center. He must see himself as the owner of the department store and as a member of the buying public. He must be able to generalize, as far as possible, from these points of view in order to strike upon the appeal or group of appeals which will be influential with as many sections of society as possible.[1]

Let us assume that our problem is the intensification in the public mind of the prestige of a hotel. The problem for the public relations counsel is to create in the public mind the close relationship between the hotel and a number of ideas that represent the things the hotel desires to stand for in the public mind.

The counsel therefore advises the hotel to make a celebration of its thirtieth anniversary which happens to fall at this particular time and suggests to the president the organization of an anniversary committee of a body of business men who represent the cream of the city's merchants. This committee is to include men who represent a number of stereotypes that will help to produce the inevitable result in the public mind. There are to be also a leading banker, a society woman, a prominent lawyer, an influential preacher, and so forth until a cross section of the city's most telling activities is mirrored in the committee. The stereotype has its effect, and what may

1. Mr. Given's definition of the qualifications of a good reporter applies very largely to the qualifications of a good public relations counsel. "There is undoubtedly a good deal of truth," says Mr. Given, "in the saying that good reporters are born and not made. A man may learn how to gather some kinds of news, and he may learn how to write it correctly, but if he cannot see the picturesque or vital point of an incident and express what he sees so that others will see as through his eyes, his productions, even if no particular fault can be found with them, will not bear the mark of true excellence; and there is, if one stops to think, a great difference between something that is devoid of faults and something that is full of good points. The quality which makes a good newspaper man must, in the opinion of many editors, exist in the beginning. But when it does exist, it can usually be developed, no mater how many obstacles are in the way."

have been indefinite impression beforehand has been reinforced and concretized. The hotel remains preeminent in the public mind. The stereotypes have proved its preeminence. The cause has been strongly presented to the public by identification with different group stereotypes.

Here is another example. A packing company desires to establish in the public mind the fact that the name of its product is synonymous with bacon. Its public relations counsel advises a contest on "Bring home the Beech-But," the contest to be open to salesman and to be based on the best sale made by salesman throughout the country during the month of August. But here again it is necessary to use a stereotype to help the possible contestant identify the cause. A committee of nationally known sales-managers is chosen to act as judges for the contest and immediately success is assured. Thousands of salesmen compete for the prize. The stereotype has bespoken the value of the contest.

The public relations counsel can try to bring about this identification by utilizing the appeals to desires and instincts discussed in the preceding chapter, and by making use of the characteristics of the group formation of society. His utilization of these basic principles will be a continual and efficient aid to him.

He must make it easy for the public to pick his issue out of the great mass of material. He must be able to overcome what has been called "the tendency on the part of public attention to 'flicker' and 'relax.'" He must do for the public mind what the newspaper, with its headlines, accomplishes for its readers.

Abstract discussions and heavy fact are the groundwork of his involved theory, or analysis, but they cannot be given to the public until they are simplified and dramatized. The refinements of reason and the shadings of emotion cannot reach a considerable public.

When an appeal to the instincts can be made so powerful as to secure acceptance in the medium of dissemination in spite of competitive interests, it can be aptly termed news.

The public relations counsel, therefore, is a creator of news for whatever medium he chooses to transmit his ideas. It is his duty to create news no matter what the medium which broadcasts this news. It is news interest which gives him an opportunity to make his idea travel and get the favorable reaction from the instincts to which he happens to appeal. News in itself we shall define later on when we discuss "relations with the press." But the word news is sufficiently understood for me to talk of it here.

In order to appeal to the instincts and fundamental emotions of the public, discussed in previous chapters, the public relations counsel must create news around his ideas. News will, by its superior inherent interest, receive attention in the competitive markets for news, which are themselves continually trying to claim the public attention. The pubic relations counsel must lift startling facts from his whole subject and present them as news. He must isolate ideas and develop them into events so that they can be more readily understood and so that they may claim attention as news.

The headline and the cartoon bear the same relation to the newspaper that the public relations counsel's analysis of a problem bears to the problem itself.

The headline is a compact, vivid simplification of complicated issues. The cartoon provides a visual image which takes the place of abstract thought. So, too, the analyses the public relations counsel makes, lift out the important, the interesting, and the easily understandable points in order to create interest.

"Yet human qualities are themselves," says Mr. Lippmann,

"vague and fluctuating. They are best remembered by a physical sign. And therefore the human qualities we tend to ascribe to the names of our impressions, themselves tend to be visualized in physical metaphors. The people of England, the history of England, condense into England, and England becomes John Bull, who is jovial and fat, not too clever, but well able to take care of himself. The migration of a people may appear to some as a meandering of a river, and to others like a devastating flood. The courage people display may be objectified as a rock, their purpose as a road, their doubts as forks of the road, their difficulties as ruts and rocks, their progress as a fertile valley. If they mobilize their dreadnaughts, they unsheath a sword. If their army surrenders they are thrown to earth. If they are oppressed they are on the rack or under the harrow."

Perhaps the chief contribution of the public relations counsel to the public and to his client is his ability to understand and analyze obscure tendencies of the public mind. It is true that he first analyzes his client's problem—he then analyzes the public mind; he utilizes the mediums of communication between the two, but before he does this he must use his personal experience and knowledge to bring two factors into alignment. It is his capacity for crystallizing the obscure tendencies of the public mind before they have reached definite expression, which makes him so valuable.

His ability to create those symbols to which the public is ready to respond; his ability to know and to analyze those reactions which the public is ready to give; his ability to find those stereotypes, individual and community, which will bring favorable responses; his ability to speak in the language of his audience and to receive from it a favorable reception are his contributions.

The appeal to the instincts and the universal desires is the basis method through which he produces his results.

PART IV

ETHICAL RELATIONS

CHAPTER I

A CONSIDERATION OF THE PRESS AND OTHER MEDIUMS OF COMMUNICATION IN THEIR RELATION TO THE PUBLIC RELATIONS COUNSEL

When the question of preparing and publishing this volume was first considered, the publishers wrote letters to several hundred prominent men asking their opinions, individually, as to the probable public interest in a work dealing with public relations. Newspaper editors and publishers, heads of large industries and public service corporations, philanthropists, university presidents and heads of schools of journalism, as well as other prominent men made up the number. Their replies are exceedingly interesting in as much as they show, almost uniformly, the increasing emphasis placed upon public relations by leaders in every important phase of American life. These replies show also a growing understanding of the need for specialized service in this field of specialized problems.

Particularly interesting were the comments of newspaper publishers and editors in response to Mr. Liveright's inquiry, for nothing could better indicate the light in which the public relations counsel is held by those very individuals who are supposed popularly to disparage his value in the social and economic scheme of things.

What are the relations of the public relations counsel to

the various mediums he can employ to carry his message to the pubic? There is, of course, first and perhaps most important, the press. There is the moving picture; the lecture platform; there is advertising; there is the direct-by-mail effort; there is the stage—drama and music; there is word of mouth; there is the pulpit, the schoolroom, the legislative chamber—to all of these the public relations counsel has distinct relationship.

The journalist of today, while still watching the machinations of the so-called "press agent" with one half-amused eye, appreciates the value of the service the public relations counsel is able to give him.

To the newspaper the public relations counsel serves as a purveyor of news.

As disseminator of news the newspaper holds an important position in American life. This has not always been the case, for the emphasis upon the news side is a development of recent years. Originally, the name newspaper was scarcely an accurate or appropriate designation for the units of the American press. So-called newspapers, were in fact, vehicles for the expression of opinion of their editors. They contained little or no news, as that word is understood today—largely because difficulties of communication made it impossible to obtain any but the most local items of interest. The public was accustomed to look to its press for the opinion of its favorite editor upon subjects of current interest rather than for the recital of mere facts.

Today, on the other hand, the expression of editorial opinion is only secondarily the function of a newspaper; and thousands of persons read newspapers with whose editorial policy they do not in the slightest agree. Such a situation would have been nearly impossible in the days of Horace Greeley.

The need which the American press is today engaged in

satisfying is the need for news. "A paper," says Mr. Given,[1] "may succeed without printing editorials worth reading and without having any aim other than the making of money, but it cannot possibly thrive unless it gests the news and prints it in a pleasing and attractive form."

Writing from a long experience with the profession of journalism, Will Irwin reaches the conclusion that[2] "news is the main thing, the vital consideration of the American newspaper; it is both an intellectual craving and a commercial need to the modern world. In popular psychology it has come to be a crying primal want of the mind, like hunger of the body. Tramp windjammers, taking on the pilot after a long cruise, ask for the papers before they ask, as formerly, for fresh fruit and vegetables. Whenever, in our later Western advance, we Americans set up a new mining camp, an editor, his type sluing on burro-back, comes in with the missionaries, evangel himself of civilization. Most dramatically the San Francisco disaster illuminated this point. On the morning of April 20, 1906, the city's population huddled in parks and squares, their houses gone, death of famine or thirst a rumor and a possibility. The editors of the three morning newspapers, expressing the true soldier spirit which inspires this most devoted profession, had moved their staffs to the suburb of Oakland, and there, on the presses of the *Tribune*, they had issued a combined *Call-Chronicle-Examiner*. When, at dawn, the paper was printed, an editor and a reporter loaded the edition into an automobile and drove it through the parks of the disordered city, giving copies away. They were fairly mobbed, they had to drive at top speed, casting out the sheets as they went,

---

1. Given, *Making A Newspaper.*
2. "What is News?" by Will Irwin, *Collier's*, March 18, 1911 (page 16).

to make any progress at all. No bread wagon, no supply of blankets, caused half so much stir as did the arrival of the news.

"We need it, we crave it; this nerve of the modern world transmits thought and impulse from the brain of humanity to its muscles; the complex organism of modern society could no more move without it than a man could move without filaments and ganglia. On the commercial and practical side, the man of even small affairs must read news in the newspapers every day to keep informed on the thousand and one activities in the social structure which affect his business. On the intellectual and spiritual side, it is—save for the Church alone—our principal outlook on the higher intelligence. The though of legislature, university, study and pulpit comes to the common man first—and usually last—in the form of news. The tedious business of teaching reading in public schools has become chiefly a training to consume newspapers. We must go far up in the scale of culture before we find an intellectual equipment more a debtor to the formal education of school and college than to the haphazard education of news."

The extent to which the editorial aspect of the newspaper has given way to an increased importance of the news columns is vividly illustrated in the anecdote about the *Philadelphia North American*, which Mr. Irwin relates. "The *North American*," says Mr. Irwin, "had declared for local option. A committee of brewers waited on the editor; they represented one of the biggest groups in their business. 'This is an ultimatum, they said. 'You must change your policy or lose our advertising. We'll be easy on you. We don't ask you to alter your editorial policy, but *you must stop printing news of local-option victories*.'[3] So the deepest and shrewdest enemies of the body politic give practi-

---

3. Italics mine.

cal testimony to the 'power of the press' in its modern form."

In the case of the brewers of Philadelphia it is my own opinion that if they had been well advised, instead of attempting to interfere with the policy of the *North American*, they would have made it a point to bring to the attention of the *North American* every instance of the defeat of local option. The newspaper would undoubtedly have published both sides of the story, as far as both sides consisted of news.

It is because he acts as the purveyor of truthful, accurate and verifiable news to the press that the conscientious and successful counsel on public relations is looked upon with favor by the journalist. And in the Code of Ethics recently adopted in Washington by a national editors' conference, his function is given acknowledgement. Just as in the case of the other mediums for the dissemination of information, mediums which range from the lecture platform to the radio, the press, too, looks to the public relations counsel for information about the causes he represents.

Since news is the newspaper's backbone, it is obvious that an understanding of what news actually is must be an integral part of the equipment of the public relations counsel. For the public relations counsel must not only supply news—he must create news. This function as the creator of news is even more important than his others.

It has always been interesting to me that a concise, comprehensive definition of news has never been written. What news is, every newspaper man instinctively knows, particularly as it concerns the needs of his own paper. But it is almost as difficult to define news as it is to describe a circular staircase without making corkscrew gestures with one's hands, or as to define some of the abstruse concepts of the metaphysician, like space or time or reality.

What is news for one newspaper may have no interest whatever, or very little interest, for another newspaper. There are almost as many definitions of news as there are journalists who take the trouble to define it. Certain of the characteristics of news, of course, can be readily seized upon; and definitions of news generally consist of particular emphasis upon one or another of these characteristics. Mr. Given remarks that[4] "news was once defined as 'Fresh information of something that has lately taken place.'…" The author of this definition puts the chief emphasis upon the elements of timeliness. Undoubtedly in most news that element must be present. It would not be true, however, to say that it must always be present, nor would it be true to say everything which is timely is news. Obviously, the well-nigh infinite number of occurrences which take place in daily life throughout the world are timely enough, so far as each of them in its respective environment is concerned; but few of them ever become news.

Mr. Irwin defines news as a "departure from the established order." Thus, according to Mr. Irwin, a criminal act is news because it is a departure from the established order, and at the same time, an exceptional display of fidelity, courage or honesty is also news for the same reason.

"With our education in established order, we get the knowledge," he says,[5] "that mankind in bulk obeys its ideals of that order only imperfectly. When something brings to our attention an exceptional adhesion to religion, virtue, and truth, that becomes in itself a departure from regularity, and therefore news. The knowledge that most servants do their work conscientiously and many stay long in the same employ is not news. But when a committee of housewives presents a

---

4. *Making a Newspaper* (page 168).
5. "What is News?" Will Irwin, *Collier's*, March 18,1911 (Page 16).

medal to a servant who has worked faithfully in one employ for fifty years, that becomes news, because it calls our attention to a case of exceptional fidelity to the ideals of established order. The fact that mankind will consume an undue amount of news about crime and disorder is only a proof that the average human being is optimistic, that he believes the world to be true, sound and working upward. Crimes and scandals interest him most because they most disturb his picture of the established order.

"That, then, is the basis of news. The mysterious news sense which is necessary to all good reporters rests on no other foundation than acquired or instinctive perception of this principle, together with a feeling for what the greatest number of people will regard as a departure form the established order. In Jesse Lynch William's newspaper play, 'The Stolen Story,' occurs this passage:

"*(Enter Very Young Reporter; comes down to city desk with air of excitement.)*

"VERY YOUNG REPORTER *(considerably impressed)*: 'Big story. Three dagoes killed by that boiler explosion!'"

"THE CITY EDITOR *(reading copy. Doesn't look up)*: 'Ten lines.' *(Continues reading copy.)*

"VERY YOUNG REPORTER *(looks surprised and hurt. Crosses over to reporter's table. Then turns back to city desk. Casual conversational tone)*'By the say. Funny thing. There was a baby carriage within fifty feet of the explosion, but it wasn't upset.'

"THE CITY EDITOR *(looks up with professional interest)*: That's worth a dozen dead dagoes. Write a half column.'

"*(Very Young Reporter looks still more surprised, perplexed. Suddenly the idea dawns upon him. He crosses over to table, sits down, writes.)*

"Both saw news; but the editor went further than the reporter. For cases of Italians killed by a boiler explosion are so common as to approach the commonplace; but a freak of explosive chemistry which annihilates a strong man and does not disturb a baby departs from it widely."

Here again it is clear that Mr. Irwin has merely emphasized one of the features generally to be found in what we call news, without, however, offering us a complete or exclusive definition of news.

Analyzing further within his general rule that news is a departure from the established order, Mr. Irwin goes on to point out certain outstanding factors which enhance or create news value. I cite them here because all of them are unquestionably sound. On the other hand, analysis shows that some of them are directly contradictory to his main principle that only the departure from the established order is news. In Mr. Irwin's opinion, the four outstanding factors making for the creation or enhancement of news value are the following:[6]

1. *"We prefer to read about the things we like."* The result, he says, has been the rule: "Power for the men, affections for the women."

2. *"Our interest in news increases in direct ration to our familiarity with its subject, its setting , and its dramatis persona."*

3. *"Our interest in news is in direct ratio to its effects on our personal concerns."*

4. *"Our interest in news increases in direct ratio to the general importance of the persons or activities which it affects."* This is so obvious that it scarcely needs comments.

---

6. What is News?" by Will Irwin, *Collier's* ,March 18, 1911 (pages 17-18). Italics mine.

Some notion of the diversity of news arising in a city may be obtained if one studies the points which are watched as news sources, either continuously or closely by metropolitan dailies. Mr. Given[7] lists the places in New York which are watched constantly:

> Police Headquarters.
> Police Courts.
> Coroner's Office.
> Supreme Courts, New York County.
> New York Stock Exchange.
> City Hall, including the Mayor's Office, Aldermanic Chamber, City Clerk's Office, and Office of the President of Manhattan Borough.
> County Clerk's office.

Those places, says Mr. Given, which the newspapers watch carefully, but not continually are:

> City Courts (Minor civil cases).
> Court of General Sessions (Criminal cases).
> Court of Special Sessions (Minor criminal cases).
> District Attorney's Office.
> Doors of Grand Jury rooms when the Grand Jury is in session (For indictments and presentments).
> Federal Courts.
> Post Office.
> United States Commissioner's Offices, and Offices of the United States Secret Service officers.
> United States Marshal's Office.
> United States District Attorney's Office.

7. *Making a Newspaper*, by Given (pages 50-62).

Ship News, where incoming and outgoing vessels are reported.

Barge Office, where immigrants land.

Surrogates Office, where wills are filed and testimony concerning wills in litigation is heard.

Political Headquarters during campaigns."

Finally, "the following are visited by the reporters several times, or only once a day:

Police Stations.
Municipal Courts.
Board of Health Headquarters.
Fire Department Headquarters.
Park Department Headquarters.
Building Department Headquarters.
Tombs Prison.
County Jail.
United States Sub-treasury.
Office of Collector of the Port.
United States Appraiser's Office.
Public Hospitals.
Leading Hotels.
The Morgue.
County Sheriff's Office.
City Comptroller's Office.
City Treasurer's Office.
Offices of the Tax Collector and Tax Assessors."

Mr. Given's example of the broker, John Smith, illustrates aptly the point I am making.

"For ten years," said Mr. Given,[8] "he pursues the even tenor of his way and except for his customers and his friends no one gives him a thought. To the newspapers he is as if he were not. But in the eleventh year he suffers heavy losses and, at last, his resources all gone, summons his lawyer and arranges for the making of an assignment. The lawyer posts off to the County Clerk's office, and a clerk there makes the necessary entries in the office docket. Here in step the newspapers. While the clerk is writing Smith's business obituary, a reporter glances over his shoulder, and a few minutes later the newspapers know Smith's troubles and are as well informed concerning his business status as they would be had they kept a reporter at his door every day for over ten years. Had Smith dropped dead instead of merely making an assignment his name would have reached the newspapers by way of the Coroner's office instead of the County Clerk's office, and in fact, while Smith did not know it, the newspapers were prepared and ready for him no matter what he did. They even had representatives waiting for him at the Morgue. He was safe only when he walked the straight and narrow path and kept quiet."

An overt act is often necessary before an event can be regarded as news.

Commenting on this aspect of the situation, Mr. Lippmann discusses this very example of the broker, John Smith, and his hypothetical bankruptcy. "That overt act," says Mr. Lippmann,[9] " 'uncovers' the news about Smith. Whether the news will be followed up or not is another matter. The point is that before a series of events become news they have usually to make themselves noticeable in some more or less overt act. Generally, too, in a crudely overt act. Smith's friends

---

8. *Making a Newspaper*, by Given (page 57).
9. *Public Opinion*, (pages 339-340).

may have known for years that he was taking risks, rumors may even have reached the financial editor if Smith's friends were talkative. But apart from the fact that none of this could be published because it would be libel, there is in these rumors, nothing definite on which to peg a story. Something definite must occur that has unmistakable form. It may be the act of going into bankruptcy, it may be a fire, a collision, an assault, a riot, an arrest, a denunciation, the introduction of a bill, a speech, a vote, a meeting, the expressed opinion of a well-known citizen, an editorial in a newspaper, a sale, a wage-schedule, a price change, the proposal to build a bridge.... There must be a manifestation. The course of events must assume a certain definable shape, and until it is in a phase where some aspect is an accomplished fact, news does not separate itself from the ocean of possible truth."

From the point of view of the practical journalist, Mr. Irwin has applied this observation to the making of the news of the day. He says:[10] "I state a platitude when I say that government by the people is the essence of democracy. In theory, the people watch and know; when, in the process of social and industrial evolution, they see a new evil becoming important, they found institutions to regulate it or laws to repress it. They cannot watch without light, know without teachers. The newspaper, or some force like it, must daily inform them of things which are shocking and unpleasant in order that democracy, in its slow, wobbling motion upward, may perceive and correct. It is good for us to know that John Smith, made crazy by drink, came home and killed his wife. Startled and shocked, but interested, we may follow the case of John Smith, see that justice in his case is not delayed by his pull with Tam-

10. "All the News That's Fit to Print," *Collier's*, May 6, 1911 (page 18).

many. Perhaps, when there are enough cases of John Smith, we shall look into the first causes and restrain the groggeries that made him momentarily mad or the industrial oppression that made him permanently an undernourished, overnerved defective. It is good to know that John Jones, a clerk, forged a check and went to jail. For not only shall we watch justice in his case, but some day we shall watch also the fraudulent race-track gambling that tempted him to theft. If every day we read of those crimes which grow from the misery of New York's East Side and Chicago's Levee, some day democracy may get at the ultimate causes for overwork, underfeeding, tenement crowding.

"No other method is so forcible with the public as driving home the instance which points the moral. General description of bad conditions fails, somehow, to impress the average mind. One might have shouted to Shreveport day after day that low dives make dangerous negroes, and created no sentiment against saloons. But when a negro, drunk on bad gin which he got at such a dive, assaulted and killed Margaret Lear, a schoolgirl, Shreveport voted out the saloon."

For the great mass of activities there is no machinery of record whatever. How these are to be recorded when they are important is the real problem for the press.

In this field the public relations counsel plays a considerable part. His is the business of calling to the public attention, through the press and through every other available medium, the point of view, the movement or the issue which he represents. Mr. Lippmann has observed that it is for this reason that what he calls the "press agent" has become an important factor in modern life.

Mr. Lippmann's observation on this point deserves comment. He says:[11] "This is the underlying reason for the existence of the press agent. This enormous discretion as to what facts and what impressions shall be reported is steadily convincing every organized group of people that whether it wishes to secure publicity or to avoid it, the exercise of discretion cannot be left to the reporter. It is safer to hire a press-agent who stands between the group and the newspapers."

The really important function of the public relations counsel, in relation to the press as well as to his client, lies even beyond these considerations. He is not merely the purveyor of news; he is more logically the *creator* of news.

An amateur can bring a good story to the average newspaper office and receive consideration, although the amateur is only too likely to miss precisely those features of his story which give it news value, and to overlook precisely that element of the story which will make it interesting to the particular newspaper he is approaching.

The New York hotel proprietors were enforcing the prohibition law in relation to their own establishments, but saw that certain restaurants were violating the law with impunity. Realizing the injustice to them of this situation, they built a definite news event by going over the heads of the local law enforcement offices and wired an appeal direct to President Harding, asking for enforcement. This naturally became news of the first order.

The opening of a shop by prominent women in which were shown graphic examples of the effect of the tariff on women's wear was an event created to intensify interest in this subject.

The launching of battleships with ceremony; the laying of corner stones; the presentation of memorials; demonstration meetings, parties and banquets are all events created with a

---

11. *Public Opinion* (page 344).

view to their carrying capacity in the various mediums that reach the public.

The departments of a modern newspaper will show the great variety of possible approaches on any subject from the standpoint of the press. When this is correlated to the possible approaches on any subject from the standpoint of human psychology, we see the diversification of methods to which the public relations counsel can have recourse to construct events.

In the metropolitan press, for instance, there are the news departments, the editorial departments, the letter-to-the-editor department, the women's department, the society department, the current events department, the sport department, the real estate department, the business department, the financial department, the shipping department, the investment department, the educational department, the photographic department and the other special feature writers and sections, different in different journals.

In a valuable study on the "Newspaper Reading Habits of Business Executives and Professional Men in New York," compiled by Professor George Burton Hotchkiss, Head of the Department of Advertising and Marketing, and Richard B. Franken, Lecturer in Advertising at New York University, there are several tables setting forth the features of morning and evening newspapers preferred as a whole by the group to whom the questionnaires were sent, and by various smaller groups within the main group.

The counsel on public relations not only knows what news value is, but knowing it, he is in the position to *make news happen*. He is a creator of events.

An organization held a banquet for a building fund to which the invitations were dispatched on large bricks. The news element in this story was the fact that bricks were dispatched.

In this capacity, as purveyor and creator of news for the press as well as for all other mediums of idea dissemination, it must be clear immediately that the public relations counsel could not possibly succeed unless he complied with the highest moral and technical requirements of those with whom he is working.

Writing on the progression of the public relations counsel, the author of an article in the *New York Times*[12] says "newspaper editors are the most suspicious and cynical of mortals, but they are as quick to discern the truth as to detect the falsehood." He goes on to discuss the particular public relations counsel whom he has in mind and whom he designates by the fictitious name Swift, and remarks: "Irrespective of their position on ethics, Swift & Co. won't deal in spurious goods. They know that one such error would be fatal. The public might forget, but the editor never. Besides, they don't have to."

Truthful and accurate must be the material which the public relations counsel furnishes to the press and other mediums. In addition, it must have the elements of timeliness and interest which are required of all news—and it must not only have these elements in general, but it must suit the particular needs of each particular newspaper and, even more than that, it must suit the needs of the particular editor in whose department it is hoped that it will be published.

Finally, the literary quality of the material must be up to the best standards of the profession of journalism. The writing must be good, in the particular sense in which each newspaper considers a story well written.

In brief, the material must come to the editorial desk as

---

11. *Times Book Review and Magazine,* January 1, 1922. "Men Who Wield the Spotlight," by Charles J. Rosebault.

carefully prepared and as accurately verified as if the editor himself had assigned a special reporter to secure and write the facts. Only by presenting his news in such form and in such a manner can the counsel on public relations hope to retain, in the case of the newspaper, the most valuable thing he possesses—the editor's faith and trust. But it must be clearly borne in mind that only in certain cases is the public relations counsel the intermediary between the news and the press. The event he has counseled upon, the action he has created finds its own lead of expression in mediums which reach the public.

The radio stations offer an avenue of approach to the public. They are controlled by private organizations, large electrical supply companies, department stores, newspapers, telegraph companies and in some cases by the government. Their programs broadcast information and entertainment to those within their radius. These programs vary in different localities.

To the public relations counsel there is a wide opportunity to utilize the means of distribution the radio affords. In partisan matters, the controllers of the radio insist upon the presentation of all points of view in order to have the onus of propaganda removed from their shoulders. The public relations counsel is therefore in a position to suggest to the broadcasting managers a symposium treatment of the subject in which he happens to be interested. Or in the case of information, which has not this partisan character, he is in a position to assure treatment of his subject by embodying his thesis in the form of a speech delivered by some individual of standing and reputation.

In the case of events which the public relations counsel may be instrumental in creating, such as large public meetings, the radio today becomes a natural form of distribution, just as news treatment in a newspaper does, and the broadcasting to thousands and thousands of people of the speeches becomes a corollary of the event itself. The broadcasting of Lord Robert Cecil's speech on the League of Nations, delivered at a banquet in New York, is a case in point.

Many magazines, for instance, are availing themselves of the radio stations to supply speeches on the particular topics they are most interested in. So the housekeeping magazines supply the radio stations with information about that phase of women's activities. The fashion magazines do likewise in their fields. And they thereby heighten their own prestige and authority in the minds of their hearers.

The use of the wireless telegraph in war time was an important factor in broadcasting information of war aims and war accomplishments to enemy countries. It was used successfully by both Allied and Central powers. It was utilized even by the Soviet Government in the announcement of its communications. This form of propagation differs slightly from the radio, referred to previously, since it depends for its efficacy not upon reaching great numbers of hearers, but upon reaching newspapers and other mediums that give currency to the material broadcasted. The wireless telegraph of course was and is a valuable asset to the public relations counsel.

The lecture platform is another well-established means of idea communication.

The spoken word has to a certain extent lost its efficacy when the lecture platform alone is considered.

The appeal of the lecture platform is limited by the actual number of those who hear the message. It is possible to reach vaster numbers through the printed word or the motion picture or even the radioed word. Both the weakness of the human voice and the physical characteristics of the place of assemblage bring about this limitation.

The lecture platform, however, still retains its importance for the public relations counsel because it affords him the opportunity to speak before group audiences which in themselves have a news value, or because it presents the opportunity to stage dramatic events that bring intensification of interest and action on the part of larger audiences than those actually addressed.

The lecture field open to the public relations counsel for the propagation of information or ideas may be divided into several classifications. First there are the lecture managers and bureaus, which act as agents in booking lecturers to different kinds of group audiences throughout the country. The public relations counsel can, for instance, suggest to his client to secure a prominent person, who because of interest in a cause will be glad to undertake a lecture tour. Then a bureau may manage the tour. The tours of important proponents on such issues as the League of Nations fall in this class as well as the tours of prominent authors, arranged by publishers in their behalf.

Then there is the lecture tour managed by the client himself and arranged through the booking of engagements with such local groups as might be interested in assuming sponsorship for what is said. A soap company might engage a lecturer on cleanliness to speak in the schools of leading communities. Or a woolen firm arrange for a home economics authority to lecture to women's clubs on dress. These speeches of course, locally, gain a wider audience than the speaker would who addressed a single meeting because they give opportunity for treatment in newspapers, advertising, circulating, and other mediums.

The lecture field offers another means of communication in as much as it gives the public relations counsel a range of group leaders to whom he can furnish the facts and ideas he is trying to propagate. The lecturers of Boards of Education in cities throughout the country, the lecturers before schools and other institutions of learning, the lecturers of one sort or another who address varied audiences can be reached directly and can become the carriers of the information the public relations counsel desires to give forth.

The meeting or public demonstration, at which prominent speakers voice their views upon the particular problem or problems at issue, would fall quite naturally under this same classification. Its main purpose, of course, is not so much to reach the audience being addressed as to make a focal point of interest for those thousands and millions who do not attend, but who get the reverberations of the speaker's voice through other mediums than their own auditory sensation.

Advertising is a medium open to the public relations counsel. In the sense in which the word is used here, the term applies to every form of paid space available for the carrying of a message. From the newspaper advertisement to the billboard, its forms are so varied that it has developed its own literature and its own principles and practice. In considering his objectives and the mediums through which his potential public can be reached the public relations counsel always considers advertising space as among his most important adjuncts. The wise public relations counsel calls into conference on the particular kinds of advertising to be used in a given problem the advertising agent who has made this study his lifework. The public relations counsel and the advertising agent then work out the problem in their respective fields.

Advertising up to the present time has laid its greatest stress upon the creation of demands and markets for specific goods. It is also applied with effectiveness to the propagation of ideas as well. It is peculiarly effective when used in combination with other methods of appeal.

Advertising controls the amount of physical space it occupies before the public eye. Advertising's dimensional qualities give it a facile flexibility that can be extended or limited at will. In a sense, too, this quality gives the special leader the opportunity to select his audience and to give them his message directly.

The field of cooperative advertising by combinations of advertisers in the same business or profession, by governments or their subdivisions, for one reason or another, is open to future possibilities.

The stage offers an avenue of approach to the public which must be regarded both from the standpoint of the numbers of individuals it reaches as well as from the circles of influence it creates by word of mouth and otherwise. To the public relations counsel therefore it offers a wide field.

Through cooperation with playwrights or managers, ideas can be given currency on the stage. When they can be translated to the action that takes place upon a stage, they are given emphasis by the visual and auditory presentation.

The motion picture falls into two fields for the purposes of t he public relations counsel. There is the field of the feature film. Here any direct utilization of the public relations counsel's ideas must come indirectly and be taken by the producer of the film from some of the other organs of thought communication. The producer may adopt for the subject of a film some idea which the public relations counsel has agitated. The film, for instance, dealing with the drug traffic came very definitely as a result of the work carried on to help relieve the drug evil.

The second field is one the public relations counsel can employ more directly. Educational films are made to order today to illustrate specific points for public consumption, from showing how product is made to showing the necessity for subway relief in a big city. These films are usually shown before a special group audience arranged for by the public relations counsel or before some other group interested in the idea the particular film stands for. Thus a Chamber of Commerce can further a film having to do with the need for better port facilities.

One phase of this kind of film is the news reel which, controlled by a private organization, films events and occasions which may have been created by the public relations counsel, but which carries because of its value in the competitve market of events.

Word of mouth is an important medium to be considered. Ideas and facts can be given currency by word of mouth. Here group leaders are strong factors in giving currency to ideas. The public relations counsel often communicates the ideas he wishes to promulgate to group leaders whose espousal of the idea he wishes to obtain.

The direct-by-mail campaign and the printed word afford the public relations counsel channels of approach to such individuals as he may desire to reach. Large companies have available for such purposes lists of individuals arranged according to innumerable criteria. There are geographical divisions, professional divisions, business divisions, and divisions of religion. There are classifications by economic position, classifications by all manner of preferences. This classification of his public into the right group for the proper appeals is one of the most important functions of the public relations counsel, as we have pointed out. The direct-by-mail method of approach offers wide opportunities for capitalizing his training and experience along these lines. Telegraphic and wireless communications would of course come under this heading.

CHAPTER II

HIS OBLIGATIONS TO THE PUBLIC AS A
SPECIAL PLEADER

It has been the history of new professions—and every pro-fession has been at some time a new profession—that they are accepted by the public and become firmly established only after two significant handicaps are overcome. The first of these, oddly enough, lies in public opinion itself; it consists of the public's reluctance to acknowledge a dependence, however slight, upon the ministrations of any one group of persons. Medicine, even today, is still fighting this reluctance. The law is fighting it. Yet these are established professions.

The second handicap is that any new profession must become established, not through the efforts and activities of others, who might be considered impartial, but through its own energy.

These handicaps are particularly potent in a profession of advocacy, because it is engaged in the partisan representa-tion of one point of view. The legal profession is perhaps the most familiar example of this fact, and in this light at least a trenchant comparison may be drawn between the bar and the new profession of the public relations counsel.

Both these professions offer to the public substantially

the same services—expert training, a highly sensitized understanding of the background from which results must be obtained, a keenly developed capacity for the analysis of problems into their constituent elements. Both professions are in constant danger of arousing crowd antagonism, because they often stand in frank and open opposition to the fixed point of view of one or another of the many groups which compose society. Indeed it is this aspect of the work of the public relations counsel which is undoubtedly the foundation of a good deal of popular disapproval of his profession.

Even Mr. Martin, who on several occasions in his volume talks with severe condemnation of what he calls propaganda, sees and admits the fundamental psychological factors which make the adherents to one point of view impute degraded or immoral motives to believers in other points of view. He says:[1]

"The crowd-man can, when his fiction is challenged, save himself from spiritual bankruptcy, preserve has defenses, keep his crowd from going to pieces, only by a demur. Any one who challenges the crowd's fictions must be ruled out of court. He must not be permitted to speak. As a witness to contrary values, his testimony must be discounted. The worth of his evidence must be discredited by belittling the disturbing witness. 'He is a bad man; the crowd must not listen to him.' His motives must be evil; he is 'bought up'; he is an immoral character; he tells lies; he is insincere or he 'has not the courage to take a stand' or 'there is nothing new in what he says.'

"Ibsen's 'Enemy of the People,' illustrates this point very well. The crowd votes that Doctor Stockman may not speak about the baths, the real point at issue. Indeed, the mayor takes the floor and officially announces that the doctor's statement that the water is bad is 'unreliable and exaggerated.' Then the

1. *The Behavior of Crowds* (pages 128-129).

president of the Householders' Association makes an address accusing the doctor of secretly 'aiming at revolution.' When finally Doctor Stockman speaks and tells his fellow citizens the real meaning of their conduct, and utters a few plain truths about 'the compact majority,' the crowd saves its face, not by proving the doctor is false but by howling him down, voting him an 'enemy of the people,' and throwing stones through the window."

If we analyze a specific example of the public relations counsel's work, we see the workings of the crowd mind, which have made it so difficult for his profession to gain popular approval. Let us take, for example, the tariff situation again. It is manifestly impossible for either side in the dispute to obtain a totally unbiased point of view as to the other side. The importer calls the manufacturer unreasonable; he imputes selfish motives to him. For his own part he identifies the establishment of the conditions upon which he insists with such things as social welfare, national safety, Americanism, lower prices to the consumer, and whatever other fundamentals he can seize upon. Every newspaper report carrying the flavor of adverse suggestion, whether on account of its facts or on account of the manner of its writing, is immediately banded as untrue, unfortunate, ill-advised. It must, the importer concludes, it must have been inspired by insidious machinations from the manufacturers' interests.

But is the manufacturer any more reasonable? If the newspapers publish stories unfavorable to his interests, then the newspapers have been "brought up," "influenced;" they are "partisan" and many other unreasonable things. The manufacturer, just like the importer, identifies his side of the struggle with such fundamental standards as he can seize upon—a living wage, reduced prices to the consumer, the American standard of employment, fair play, justice. To each the contentions of the other are untenable.

Now, carry this situation one step further to the point at which the public relations counsel is retained, on behalf of one side or the other. Observe how sincerely each side and its adherents call even the verifiable facts and figures of the other by that dread name "propaganda." Should the importers submit figures showing that wages could be raised and the price to the consumer reduced, their adherents would be gratified that such important educational work should be done among the public and that the newspapers should be so fair-minded as to publish it. The manufacturers, on the other hand, will call such material "propaganda" and blame either the newspaper which publishes those figures or the economist who compiled them, or the public relations counsel who advised collating the material.

The only difference between "propaganda" and "education," really, is in the point of view. The advocacy of what we believe in is education. The advocacy of what we don't believe in is propaganda. Each of these nouns carries with it social and moral implications. Education is valuable, commendable, enlightening, instructive. Propaganda is insidious, dishonest, underhand, misleading. It is only today that the viewpoint on this question is undergoing a slight change, as the following editorial would indicate:

"The relativity of truth,"[2] says Mr. Elmer Davis, "is the commonplace to any newspaper man, even to one who has never studied epistemology; and, if the phrase is permissible, truth is rather more relative in Washington than anywhere else. Now and then it is possible to make a downright statement; such and such a bill has passed in one of the houses of

---

2. *History of the New York Times* (pages 279-380).

Congress, or failed to pass; the administration has issued this or that statement; the President has approved, or vetoed, a certain bill. But most of the news that comes out of Washington is necessarily rather vague, for it depends on the assertions of statesman who are reluctant to be quoted by name, or even by description. This more than anything else is responsible for the sort of fog; the haze of miasmatic exhalations, which hangs over news with a Washington date line. News coming out of Washington is apt to represent not what is so but what might be so under certain contingencies, what may turn out to be so, what some eminent personage says is so, or even what he wants the public to believe is so when it is not."

Most subjects on which there is so-called definite public opinion are much more vague and indefinite, much more complex in their facts and in their ramifications than the news from Washington which the historian of the *New York Times* describes. Consider, for example, what complicated issues are casually disposed of by the average citizen. An uninformed lay public may condemn a new medical theory on slight consideration. Its judgment is hit or miss, as medical history proves.

Political, economic and moral judgments, as we have seen, are more often expressions of crowd psychology and herd reaction than the result of the calm exercise of judgment. It is difficult to believe that this is not inevitable. Public opinion in a society consisting of millions of persons, all of whom must somehow or other reach a working basis with most of the others, is bound to find a level of uniformity founded on the intelligence of the average member of society as a whole or of the particular group to which one may belong. There is a different set of facts on every subject for each man. Society cannot wait to find absolute truth. It cannot weigh every issue carefully before making a judgment. The result is that the so-called truths by which society lives are born of compromise among conflicting desires and of interpretation by many minds. They are accepted and intolerantly maintained once they have been determined. In the struggle among ideas, the only test is the one which Justice Holmes of the Supreme Court pointed out—the power of thought to get itself accepted in the open competition of the market.

The only way for new ideas to gain currency is through the acceptance of them by groups. Merely individual advocacy will leave the truth outside the general fund of knowledge and beliefs. The urge toward suppression of minority or dissentient points of view is counteracted in part by the work of the public relations counsel.

The standards of the public relations counsel are his own standards and he will not accept a client whose standards do not come up to them. While he is not called upon to judge the merits of his case any more than a lawyer is called upon to judge his client's case, nevertheless he must judge the results which his work would accomplish from an ethical point of view.

In law, the judge and jury hold the deciding balance of power. In public opinion, the public relations counsel is judge and jury because through his pleading of a case the public is likely to accede to his opinion and judgment. Therefore, the public relations counsel must maintain an intense scrutiny of his actions, avoiding the propagation of unsocial or otherwise harmful movements or ideas.

Every public relations counsel has been confronted with the necessity of refusing to accept clients whose cases in a law court would be valid, but whose cases, in the higher court of public opinion are questionable.

The social value of the public relations counsel lies in the fact that he brings to the public facts and ideas of social utility which would not so readily gain acceptance otherwise. While he, of course, may represent men and individuals who have already gained great acceptance in the public mind, he may represent new ideas of value which have not yet reached their point of largest acceptance or greatest saturation. That in itself renders him important.

As for the relations between the public relations counsel and his client, little can be said which would not be merely a repetition of that code of decency by which men and women make moral judgments and live reputable lives. The public relations counsel owes his client conscientious, effective service, of course. He owes to his client all the duties which the professions assume in relation to those they serve. Much more important than any positive duty, however, which the public relations counsel owes to his client is the negative duty—that he must never accept a retainer or assume a position which puts his duty to the groups he represents above his duty to his own standards of integrity—to the larger society within which he lives and works.

Europe has given us the most recent important study of public opinion and its social and historical effects. It is interesting because it indicates the sweep of the development of an international realization of what a momentous factor in the world's life public opinion is becoming. I feel that this paragraph from a recent work of Professor Van Ferdinand Tonnies is of particular significance to all who would feel that the conscious moulding of public opinion is a task embodying high ideals.

"The future of public opinion," says Professor Tonnies, "is the future of civilization. It is certain that the power of public opinion is constantly increasing and will keep on increasing.

It is equally certain that it is more and more being influenced, changed, stirred by impulses from below. The danger which this development contains for a progressive ennobling of human society and a progressive heightening of human culture is apparent. The duty of the higher strata of society—the cultivated, the learned, the expert, the intellectual—is therefore clear. They must inject moral and spiritual motives into public opinion. Public opinion must become public conscience."

It is in the creation of a public conscience that the counsel on public relations is destined, I believe, to fulfill his highest usefulness to the society in which he lives.